Mary Hite's *Story*

To Byron Park friends

Joe Fox

A PIONEER WOMAN WITH GRIT

By Joseph M. Fox

STRATTON
—PRESS—
Publishing Life

MARY HITE'S
Copyright © 2019 **Joseph M. Fox**

Stratton Press Publishing
831 N Tatnall Street Suite M #188,
Wilmington, DE 19801
www.stratton-press.com
1-888-323-7009

ISBN (Paperback): 978-1-64345-623-2
ISBN (Hardback): 978-1-64345-628-7
ISBN (Ebook): 978-1-64345-816-8

Printed in the United States of America

MARY HITE'S STORY

My earlier book, *Growing with America: Colonial Roots*, was a compendium of new genealogical and genetic family research. Although it did achieve that purpose, casual readers might be turned off by the mere volume of information. Buried within it were a number of fascinating personal stories and I've chosen one that I feel deserves more attention.

From a well-known frontier family with famous connections, Mary Hite lived through the American Revolution and the War of 1812, outlasted two husbands and, in an era when men dominated, was able to pretty much chart her own course. In those days, married women had few legal rights and were dependent on their men-folk for almost everything. Mary Hite was an exception. Her story also tells how diverse traditions and religious inclinations came together in Washington, DC, right as it became our nation's capital. This had a huge effect on some of Mary's descendants.

As far as facts are concerned, the Memoirs of Jonathan Roberts[i] and the letters of Edward Fitzgerald in the Doyle Collection at the Virginia Historical Society[ii] cover the last four years of Mary's life in considerable detail. Her earlier life is less well defined but enough new documentation has been uncovered that, along with the known history of the times, a fairly detailed account can be made. Obviously, it has been necessary to use a little imagination and a timeline of known facts is provided

MARY'S FAMILY
BACKGROUND

Jacob Hite (1718–1776), the father of Mary Hite, was born in Perkiomen, Chester County, Pennsylvania, and died at the hands of Cherokee Indians in South Carolina. His father and mother were Hans Joost (or Justus) Heydt (1685–1761) and Anna Maria Merkle (1686–1769) of Bonfield, Heilbronn, Baden-Wuerttemberg, Germany.[1] They immigrated to New York State, moved to Bucks County, Pennsylvania, and eventually ended up living at *Long Meadows*, Frederick County, Virginia, near Winchester. Frederick County, as it was then called, is now divided into Berkeley, Hampshire, Hardy, Morgan and Jefferson Counties in West Virginia, plus Clarke, Frederick, Shenandoah and Warren Counties in Virginia.

Once in America, Joost Heydt changed his name to Jost Hite. Originally a linen weaver, Jost and his family, consisting of his wife, four daughters and his father, Johannes, emigrated to Kingston in New York State along with other Palatine families in 1709. He spent some time in New York as an Indian fur trader but soon moved to Pennsylvania, first on the Skippack River near Germantown and then, in 1718, to the Perkiomen River where Jost built a grist mill and prospered. Here, five sons were born.

---

1   Some researchers have identified his wife as Anna Maria Du Bois.

Always ready for a new venture, Jost heard from Jacob Van Meter of very promising unsettled land in a valley located beyond the Blue Ridge Mountains of Virginia. Governor Spotswood had explored this land back in 1716. It was still Indian territory, though the Indians used it primarily as a thoroughfare, on trails following the north-flowing river they called the Shenandoah. Hite and his partners acquired rights to 140,000 acres with the stipulation that they settle one family per thousand acres within a two-year period. He sold the grist mill and property in Pennsylvania to help finance the deal and the grist mill eventually became known as the Pennypacker Mill.

A party of fifteen families, led by Jost Hite, set off by wagon train in 1731 for that undeveloped area in Virginia. They had to cut their own roads for part of the trip and they became the primary white settlers west of the Blue Ridge Mountains.

There was plenty of hardwood available for building and the land had an excellent mix of tillable loam and minerals such as lime to improve the soil. It was good for both grazing and farming and eventually became the prime farmland of Virginia.[iii] Rapidly selling off parcels of land, Jost became very rich, acquiring the moniker "Baron of the Shenandoah." There was a land controversy, however. Lord Fairfax, who lived in Virginia, had been promised much of the land by the British Crown and claimed almost everything. Jost Hite fought for his property rights legally and after his death, the Hites won the battle.

Jost settled where Opequan Creek crossed the main route down the valley and built a tavern and mill just south of what became the town of Winchester, Virginia.[2] The creek flows north from this point—parallel to the Shenandoah River—and enters the Potomac about twenty miles upstream of Harpers Ferry, which is located where the Shenandoah merges with the Potomac.

Before settlers arrived, most of the valley appears to have been a route that the Shawnee, Seneca, Catawba, Delaware and other Indian tribes traveled through and hunted but did not claim as their

---

2   There were many changes in county and state boundaries in the 1700s. Frederick County, Virginia, was formed from Orange County in 1743 and Winchester was made its capital. West Virginia became a state during the Civil War.

own, though the Shawnee had villages near what became Winchester, Virginia, and Moorefield, West Virginia. Jost Hite and Jacob Van Meter had many peaceful dealings with Shawnee tribesmen but around 1754, the Shawnee moved west. The French and Indian Wars had commenced and this area was at the edge of the conflict. Colonel George Washington built Fort Loudoun in Winchester in 1756 to protect the area. He built six more forts westward in Hampshire County, which was the scene of many hostilities.

Hite's initial purchase of 40,000 acres from Jacob Van Meter covered most of the Opequan Creek watershed. He immediately started looking for sites for his married daughters and for his five sons as they grew older. The daughters had married men named Bowman, Froman and Chrisman. They were eventually raising families all over the valley and even into the hills of Hampshire County to the west. His eldest son John was married in 1737, building next to his father, and eventually taking over the mill and hostelry. The John Hite Mansion, called Springdale, is shown in figure 1. It has been put in pristine condition but on the same property are the ruins of Jost Hite's Fort, shown in figure 2.

Figure 1
Springdale: Home of John Hite

Figure 2
Ruins of Jost Hite's Fort

Jost built a house for his third son, Isaac, about six miles south of Winchester, near the present village of Middletown. This was a prime farming location and Isaac developed a prosperous plantation called Long Meadows. Jost moved there himself in 1737 and his first wife, Anna Marie Merkle, died there in 1738. Jost remarried in 1741 but had no more children.

The next son, Abraham, moved west and married Rebecca Van Meter. They lived at Fort Pleasant on the South Branch of the Potomac River in Hampshire County. Rebecca's father, Isaac van Meter, lived nearby. They were the family members most exposed to Indian raids but all the Hites were wary of Indians, particularly during the early days of the war in 1756 and 1757.

Jost's second son, Jacob, elected to build thirty miles north in the Opequan watershed on a stream called Hopewell Run in what is now Jefferson County, West Virginia. In 1741, when he was twenty and she nineteen, Jacob married Catherine O'Bannon whose Irish father lived in Virginia's Northern Neck, near Alexandria. A few years after his marriage, Jacob built the stone house called Hopewell and moved there, putting up a mill and building a fort for defense against the Indians.

The youngest, Joseph, settled near Jacob Hite, was married and had a child but died soon after that.

1754–1771

Childhood at Hopewell

Mary was born at Hopewell, her father's 2,700-acre estate on Hopewell Run, either in 1753 or the first two months of 1754.[3] This area is now called Leetown in what became Berkeley County, West Virginia, in 1772, and Jefferson County, in 1801. A lot of development had occurred since her grandfather, Jost Hite, had brought his family here in 1731.

Life at Hopewell for Mary must have been very confusing and she may have felt neglected at times. She was the fourth of five children—three boys and two girls—the oldest being thirteen years older than she. Her father also adopted his nephew, Joseph Hite Jr., when Joseph's father and mother died near Hopewell in 1758. In addition to the six kids, there were many slaves around doing work as menials, craftsmen or laborers. Her father had arranged for a teacher to come and give lessons to the kids. There was always something to keep the kids busy.

Jacob, Mary's father, was always doing something a little different and was away a lot. He had been only thirteen when the family moved to Virginia but quickly took on the job of finding

---

3   Her obituary gives her age as sixty-four when she died in February 1818.

new settlers from Ireland and Scotland. Also involved in commercial trade, he had a part interest in the brigantine *Swift* and the schooner *Friendship*, which were kept at Alexandria, Virginia, the nearest open-water port. He owned property there near the waterfront and that was probably where he met his first wife.

On the other hand, there was plenty of room for children to play and plenty of playmates, though you always had to be on the lookout for Indians. The French and Indians Wars had started in about the same year that she was born.

Mary's first lasting memories, however, were the death of her mother, Catherine, when she was seven years old and that of her German grandfather, Jost Hite, when she was eight. The Hite family and their friends, and there were plenty of them, gathered at Long Meadows in 1761 to mourn their patriarch.[4] What she remembered most was being overwhelmed by a host of aunts and uncles and playing with numerous young cousins. Jost Hite had many friends including his fellow Virginians, George Washington and Thomas Jefferson, as well as the Madison family.

It was surely at this gathering that Jacob Hite found his second wife, the widowed Frances Madison Beale, and they were married in December of 1761. Frances had a young nephew named James Madison, three years older than Mary, who later became the fourth president of the United States. James could well have been at the funeral but was very shy and hard to get to know.

Living farther north, Mary had been a bit isolated from many of the cousins she was now meeting. But this changed when Frances Madison brought along her five Beale children from Orange County to Hopewell. Ranging in age from six to sixteen, they were roughly the same age as the five Hite children, and they became a very close-knit family unit. While Mary Hite, her brother James and Annie Beale were playing hide-and-seek in their father's fort, the older children were falling in love. Only two years later, in December 1763, Mary's sister Betty married her oldest stepbrother, Taverner Beale Jr. Nine years later, Mary's brother Thomas married his oldest stepsister,

---

4   This gathering is purely fictional but seems a likely event.

Frances Madison Beale. You have to believe that Mary's stepmother was somehow involved in all of this matchmaking.

Mary later became an accomplished letter writer, schoolteacher and businesswoman but where did she get her education? Much of this may have rubbed off from her brothers and male cousins who went off to college but one of Jost and Jacob Hite's goals in recruiting settlers was to find schoolteachers. John Willson was a Scots-Irish immigrant, recruited by Jost in 1737, who was the first schoolteacher in Winchester and also led Presbyterian chapel services until visiting ministers appeared. Undoubtedly, Jacob Hite did something similar to bring education to Leetown and to provide schooling for his children.

There was always something happening at the Jacob Hite residence and life there got pretty hectic after Mary became a teenager. In the late 1760s, Jacob Hite got into a large land deal on Cherokee lands in South Carolina, a back-door deal that turned sour when a British official intervened. When his deed was voided, Jacob was seriously in debt and the Berkeley sheriff—a man named Stephens—came and appropriated some of his slaves and horses to put them up for auction. Jacob, of course, resisted and was aided by his son Thomas. By the late summer of 1772, creditors were trying to force him to sell off a large portion of his Hopewell land and slaves.[iv] Over the next few years, his properties in Alexandria were sold to pay off his debts. The hounding only stopped when Sheriff Stephens went off to war.

On March 7, 1770, Jacob Hite prepared a will,[v] dividing his estate equally among his four sons with a life estate to his wife Frances of one quarter after selling property to pay debts and provide for his daughters. Frances and his sons John and Thomas were named executors, along with a man named James Keith. Mary, then sixteen, was given "the lands and plantations on Opequon bought of Joseph Beeler[vi] whereon now live Benjamin Wittell, Benjamin Wallingsford, Widow Craven, Thomas Ball, John Gooding and Widow Leister or one thousand pounds current money of Virginia at the choice of my said daughter."

On December 21, 1771, a codicil was added to provide clothing and schooling for his underage children. Jacob's will was not proven until March 16, 1779, well after his death, when his son Thomas Hite and several witnesses presented it to the Berkeley County Court.

The bequest of land to Mary was really quite unusual. Jacob's other daughters were only given money. Did her father recognize some unusual capabilities in this daughter of his or did he feel she might need some additional help financially? Perhaps both. In any case, she could not have received the property until 1779 at the earliest, by which time, much had happened to change the whole situation.

1772-1777

A Minister's Wife

At age seventeen, Mary was betrothed to Nathaniel Manning, a prospective Anglican Minister from New Jersey, sixteen years older than she. As we've seen, this was a turbulent and unsettled time for the Jacob Hite family and it was natural for Mary to look for some sort of security. Her brother Thomas and stepsister Frances were already talking of marrying each other. There is little question, however, that Mary's was an arranged marriage.

Mary was growing up and her stepmother, who already had a reputation as a matchmaker, had begun looking around for potential husbands. Uncle Abraham Hite reported that his frontier Hampshire Parish was looking for a permanent minister. In response to such demands, the Anglican Church was sending three men over to England in 1771 to be ordained since there were no bishops in America to perform this sacrament. One of these three men was Nathaniel Manning, nine years out of Princeton. He had been practicing medicine in New Jersey, near Philadelphia, but had decided to become an Episcopalian minister. Frances Hite's nephew, James Madison, was then attending Princeton and knew of Nathaniel. What better combination of talents for a frontier parish? He was looking for a wife to accompany him and Mary's name was suggested.

Nathaniel had a sister living near the Hites whom he could consult. The families of Margaret Manning and Beniah Martin had a long history of living near each other in Piscataway Township, New Jersey.[vii] The two had married in 1764, probably back in New Jersey, but were now living in Berkeley County, Virginia, and had several young sons.[viii] They could assure Nathaniel that Mary Hite was a pretty, precocious and perky lass who stood to inherit a fortune.

Things had to move rapidly since he was to leave for England for indoctrination and ordination, so any visit he paid to Mary's family must have been very quick indeed. What a way to meet your future husband! They could have talked about many things and we can only speculate on a few.

Mary could see that Nathaniel was very dedicated to his newly adopted religion and that was all right with her. Anyone headed for a frontier parish would have to be dedicated. When Mary went to church, this was the one she attended. Up to now, religion had never been an issue with the Hites. Her family was a mixture of German Lutherans and Irish Protestants most of whom had switched to the more socially elite Anglican faith. Frontier America was pretty tolerant of different religions, though the state of Virginia considered the Anglican Episcopal Church its official religion and Anglican vestrymen were responsible for social order.[ix] Her Hite uncles were all Anglican vestrymen as befit their social standing and this was her stepmother's religion.

There were troubles brewing between England and the Colonies. Ben Franklin was then in London and was beginning to have serious doubts about a Royal Government for America. Nathaniel had heard rumors of this in Philadelphia and Jacob wondered if this could lead to trouble.

"No," said Nat, "Franklin will surely bring the British around to our way of thinking."

Nathaniel was serious and a bit stodgy but did seem a truly good man and since Mary really had little choice, they agreed to marry as soon as he would get back from London.

By late April or May 1772, Nathaniel had returned from England.[5] The other two ministers sent to England with him never got near Hampshire County but Nathaniel kept his word. After all, he had an attractive woman waiting for him. Perhaps they were able to stay for the marriage of Thomas Hite and Frances Beale, her brother and stepsister, in November, but certainly, they were themselves married and off to Hampshire County by the end of 1772. Jacob Hite was beginning to get rid of his properties in Berkeley County in 1772 and he deeded 842 acres to Mary and her new husband, the Reverend Nathaniel Manning, as a wedding present.[x]

He was thirty-four and she was only eighteen when they set up housekeeping in Hampshire County at The Glebe, just north of the present town of Moorefield. This was the name given to property maintained by the County, which served as residence and source of income for the pastor. The area encompassed by his parish covered the present counties of Hampshire, Hardy, Mineral and Grant and part of Pendleton and Mineral.[xi] Now part of West Virginia, this was then Virginia land that George Washington had surveyed for Lord Fairfax as a young man and much of it was still under Fairfax control.

Nancy Schultz in *Mrs. Mattingly's Miracle* gives a description of that area that is very revealing:[xii]

"Moorefield was settled over what Native Americans considered hallowed ground. Their graveyard had been laid out on the floodplain of the river junction, 820 feet above sea level, where the town was located. Two ancient trails—the Seneca and what later became known as the McCullough trader's trail, both followed the paths of rivers and crossing the Allegheny divide— also intersected at this plateau. Native Americans had long buried their dead at the crossroads, and the gravesites stretched down to the riverbanks. In the western third of what is now Hardy County, West Virginia, the Moorefield River flows into the south branch of the Potomac. Native Americans cleared large fields for planting in the middle of forests. Well into the twentieth century, these clearings were still called 'Indian Old Fields.'

---

5   Anglican church documents say his ship left England in March.

"Moorefield's limestone soil, rich with Indian bones, arrowheads, and pottery shards, was well suited to growing grass for grazing, corn, and tobacco. As the settlers plowed and built on the floodplain, the ground spit up reminders of the past. A highly finished pipe, with the figure of a snake coiled round the bowl, its head peering over the brim, was found on the riverbank. A human jawbone of enormous size was discovered nearby, with peculiar, prehistoric teeth. It seemed that giants had once roamed this land. This awareness of a long past was woven into the Indian names given to places in the town and perhaps contributed to a culture of tolerance unusual for its day. The 1790 census, for example, lists 411 free, nonwhite people, 42 more than the 369 slaves in the county. At the turn of the nineteenth century, Hardy was apparently the only county in Virginia that had more free black people than slaves. Most of these were likely freed or escaped slaves from Virginia who made their way up the Potomac River Valley to the mountainous border country. People of African origins living in Hardy County could see that more than half of their number had escaped the chains of slavery. To the nineteenth-century mind, Moorefield was a town wrested from savages and reclaimed from the wilderness. The dangers and attractions of the frontier lay to the west. This borderland enticed nonconformists seeking freedom and individual expression in the vast wilderness spaces."

Did they really know what they were getting into? The pastor's life in those remote parishes was not an easy one. Nathaniel needed to be away from home a lot while tending to his far-flung flock. For Mary, there was one saving grace. Abraham Hite, and the other vestrymen for Hampshire Parish, had found a location for The Glebe at Lot No. 5 in South Branch Manor[6] that was reasonably close to his own residence near Old Fields.[xiii] Lot 1 in South Branch Manor was right below The Trough, that seven-mile gorge carved into the Allegheny Mountains

---

6   A Fairfax development.

by the South Branch of the Potomac River as it flows north toward the town of Romney. The lot numbers increased as you went south. Abraham Hite's 668-acre lot was Number 2. The Hardy Glebe is listed as Lot Number 5 at 210 acres, which would put it perhaps a mile south of there. At least, Mary would have some family nearby.

The Hites actually lived at Fort Pleasant on property Rebecca had inherited from her father, Isaac Van Meter, who had died in 1757. Lord Fairfax had also claimed this land but Van Meter, like Jost Hite, had fought him off. One of the string of forts established by Washington in 1756, Fort Pleasant is also known to have been close to the entrance to The Trough.

Where was Fort Pleasant actually located? Figure 3 gives the most probable answer. A map, hand-drawn in May 1770, by Thomas Witt shows the fort to be located on about one and a half acres near the confluence of Pleasant Creek and Grassy Creek and surrounded by Abraham Hite land to the southwest across Grassy Creek and Van Meter land to the east. *The History of Hardy County*[7] says the fort was "built on the bottom land northeast of the point where Anderson Run flows into Mudlick Run and on the northeast bank of Mudlick Run. It was a substantial fortification. The stockade enclosed about an acre and a half of ground. The main gate was in the north wall facing the Trough and blockhouses were constructed at each of the four corners of the stockade. Inside the stockade were huts or barracks, stables, a powder magazine, officers' cabin and commissary cabin. Several small log buildings were outside the stockade."

Comparing the 1770 map with a present-day satellite map of the area, it is concluded that Pleasant Creek is now called Mudlick Run and Grassy Creek is now Anderson Run. The location is off Reynold's Gap Road one half mile east of the present tiny village of Old Fields. Most of the area is now under cultivation but there is a barn right about where the fort would have been located. The village of Old Fields is on US 220 about five miles northwest of the town of Moorefield, West Virginia. Moorefield is now the capital of Hardy County, West Virginia.

---

7   Pages 38 and 39.

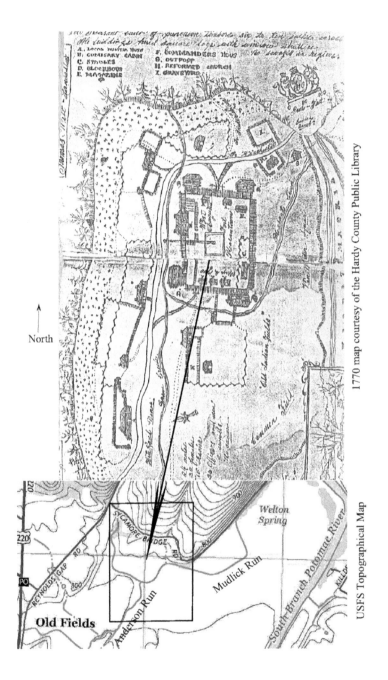

North

1770 map courtesy of the Hardy County Public Library

USFS Topographical Map

Figure 3

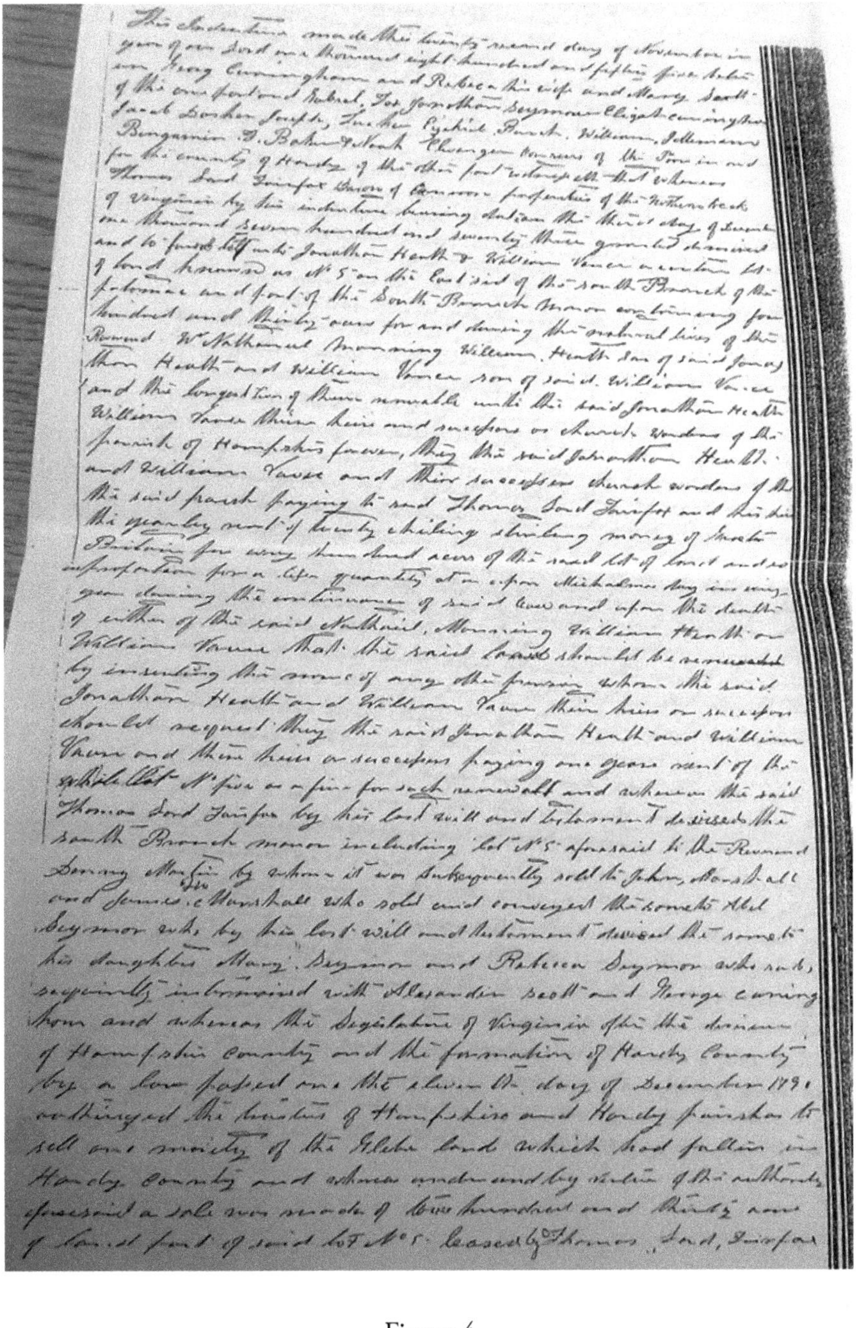

Figure 4
Page 1 of the Poor Farm Deed

A remarkable 1855 Poor Farm deed, figure 4, available in the Hardy County Library, describes the location of Lot 5 in the South Branch Manor and clearly identifies Reverend Manning[8] and church wardens, Jonathan Heath and William Vance, as the lessees of The Glebe from Lord Fairfax in 1773. This property later became the Poor Farm. Heath and Vance were paying Lord Fairfax an annual rental of 20 shillings per hundred acres and the property is described as including 430 acres. It is on the other side of the river from Fort Pleasant and the reported location of the Poor Farm places it three miles due south of Fort Pleasant on Smoky Hollow Road. Sons of Heath and Vance were also residing there and farming the land.

How easy was it for Mary to visit her Hite cousins? Using present-day roads, it would take 1 hour and 25 minutes to walk the 4.3 miles as shown figure 5 (next page). In Mary's day, there was no bridge but there are several low areas on the South Branch that are good places for a horse and rider or horse and buckboard to ford the river. Most likely, she took a horse and followed an old wagon road north that later became Trough Road, fording the river opposite Fort Pleasants where there was a good fording place to accommodate traffic to the fort. It was a precarious trip, however, at the wrong time of year—spring thaw or heavy rains. Once upset, you were swept downriver into the Trough. A descendant of the Poor Farm manager reports that several of her ancestors died while attempting to ford the river.

So this is where Mary and Nathaniel were living starting in 1772. One can imagine one of his parishioners riding up to The Glebe on a foam-flecked horse with the news that little Johnny was doing poorly with a high fever. "Could the doctor come quickly?" Here was a pastor who could do double duty. The first year was a challenge for both of them, learning the customs and the territory.

Figure 3 shows a Reformed Church and graveyard next to the Van Meter property. Was this to become Rev. Nathaniel Manning's home church? We really don't know. There was once an Anglican church about a mile south of Moorefield and that's another possibility. With all that territory to cover, he must have been on the road a great deal of the time.

---

8   He is called Reverend Wm Nathaniel Manning, the only known document where the name William occurs.

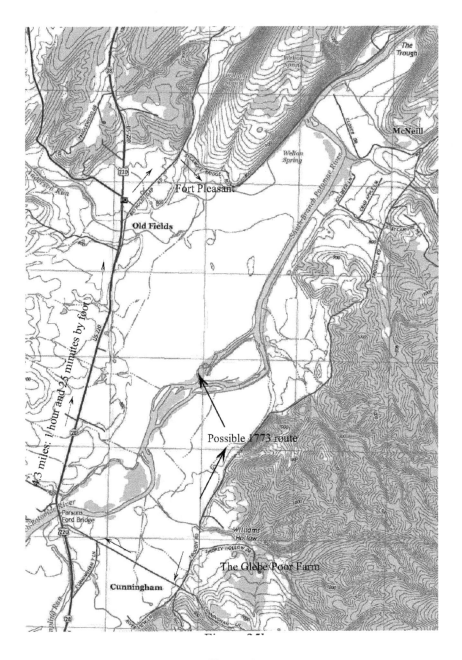

Figure 5
Topographic Map of the Northern Area of South Branch Manor

Mary not only had to adjust to the role of a minister's wife but to the absence of her own family when her father—fed up with local politics—decided to take his family to South Carolina in 1773.

Her Uncle Abraham was also away a lot—scouting out land in Kentucky and serving in the Virginia Assembly—but his wife, Rebecca, was around to help Mary as her children were born. Rebecca had four sons and a daughter. Isaac, the oldest, was a year older than Mary and all of them were itching to move westward into frontier Kentucky territory. xiv

In 1773, Isaac was out surveying lands in Kentucky and his father and his brother, Abraham Jr., had accompanied him part of the time. In the summer and fall of 1774, following another surveying expedition, Isaac led a group of six men on a canoe trip down the Ohio and Mississippi Rivers to New Orleans, returning home by ship in December.xv He must have passed by The Glebe on his way home and Mary was fascinated by his story.

"There are vast stretches of land out west to be settled and huge rivers to be crossed," Ike told her, "it is all Indian land but open to be conquered."

In the fall of 1775, Abraham Hite was out in Kentucky again with his sons Isaac and Abraham and a couple of their Bowman cousins, surveying and laying claims to land on a creek just above the Falls of the Ohio. This would be in the heart of what is now Louisville.

It must have been a pretty lonely existence for Mary and on a preacher's earnings (typically 16,000 pounds of tobacco plus rentals on the *Glebe*), they could not have afforded much in the way of help. Possibly Mary had brought along a slave or two to help. This was the way things were done in those days, though there is no such indication of a slave in Nathaniel's will. Her father is known to have had as many as 210 slaves and took them with him when he moved south. But Moorefield and Hardy County had developed a tolerance for black people that was really quite unusual. This must have had its effect on the Hites, the Van Meters and Mannings.[9]

---

9   This was brought to the fore in the PBS television series *African American Lives 2* (2008) where it was revealed that, in 1823, Abraham van Meter freed

Reverend Manning's tenure occurred during a tricky time for the Anglicans. When Nathaniel started ministering, the Colonies were in an uproar in reaction to the Boston Tea Party and this, somewhat belatedly, reached even into Hampshire County. The frontier sensed war coming with Britain and many Anglicans were Loyalists at a time when that was becoming very unpopular.

At the same time, there were many voices supporting freedom of religion and abolishing state-sponsored churches. Members of other religions[10] in Hampshire Parish were becoming fed up with the requirement that they support the Anglican Church financially and were organizing a petition against doing so.[xvi]

Indians could also be a problem. The Shawnee and other Indian tribes were very upset with their treatment out in Kentucky County, Virginia, along the Ohio River, culminating in Lord Dunmore's War in 1774. Settlers back in the Allegheny Mountains always had to be on the alert.

The Manning's first child, Jacob Hite Manning, came along just as summer began in 1774. Her doctor-husband delivered the baby and Mary nursed it through the summer. Parish duties kept her husband away a lot but Mary did have the two sons of vestrymen, William Heath and William Vance, to keep an eye on her as they farmed The Glebe. And Rebecca Hite could help during those first difficult weeks.

Mary was beginning to enjoy her situation and things went along reasonably smoothly the whole next year until she learned she was pregnant again in the summer of 1775. She then decided to visit relatives in Shenandoah County for the birth of her second child. It may just have been a desire for family help and reassurance but one also wonders about the health of her husband whose job was

---

Joe and Sarah Bruce, great-great-great-great-grandparents of Professor Henry Louis Gates, the producer of the series. This appears to have been in Hardy County.

10 *The Ten Thousand Name Petition* presented to the House of Delegates in October 1776 was essentially a Baptist petition. They said they had "long groaned under the Burden of an Ecclesiastical Establishment" and asked that "this as well as every other Yoke may be broken, and the oppressed may go free" with "every religious Denomination being on a level."

proving a difficult one. She talked it over with Nathaniel and he agreed that she should leave right away. This was a difficult trip for a pregnant woman carrying a year-old baby, the trail going over several high passes. It would have been impossible in the middle of winter. Fortunately, there were Bowman cousins frequently coming through Fort Pleasant on their way to explore Kentucky territory,[11] and one of them offered to accompany her on the journey. This trip, perhaps, was why her brother John deeded to her a riding chair and horse in his will, written later that year.[xvii]

She probably was staying with her sister, Elizabeth, and her husband, Taverner Beale, Jr., who lived in Shenandoah County but this was also home for her Bowman cousins who lived right on the northern border of the county. There was a Hite enclave stretching from there north to Winchester so she was well supplied with family even though there was a war going on. Nathaniel Manning Jr. was born on January 12, 1776, and his baptism was recorded on March 20 in Shenandoah County.[xviii]

The Revolutionary War was underway by then and most young male members of the Hite clan were in Washington's army. This included Mary's older brother, Major Thomas Hite, her Fort Pleasant cousin Captain Abraham Hite Jr., and Major Isaac Hite Jr., her eighteen-year-old cousin from Long Meadow, just out of college at William and Mary. Her half-brother George Hite was just fifteen and a student at William and Mary College when he, too, went off to war.

Things had gone well so far but then calamities began to strike. Mary got notice that her father and most of his family in South Carolina had been massacred by Indians only a few days before the Declaration of Independence was proclaimed in Philadelphia. Always looking for an opportunity to help, Jacob Hite had been trying to negotiate peace with the Indians when they savagely turned against him. He, his wife, Frances, and his son, Jacob Jr., were killed by Cherokee Indians in 1776, possibly in trying to win them over to the side of the revolution. A memorial marker was installed there in

---

11   This is an assumption but some of the Bowman boys had been out in Kentucky with Abraham Hite and his sons, so Mary knew them well.

2009 (see figure 6).[12] The exact fate of two young daughters, Eleanor and Susan, and a number of slaves remains a mystery to this day though it is suspected that they were carried off and adopted by the Cherokee Indian tribe.

Hite Massacre Historical Marker Unveiled

Descendants of Frances Madison Beale Hite (President Madison's aunt) and her second husband Jacob Hite, along with representatives from Sons of the American Revolution, Daughters of the American Revolution, Society of Colonial Wars and Colonial Dames attended the unveiling of a state historical marker near Greer, South Carolina on Dec. 8, 2009 which marks the spot of Hite homestead and massacre of the family that took place at the hands of the Cherokee on July 1, 1776. Thought to have been incited by British sympathizers hostile to the Hites who had established a thriving and prosperous trading center in the South Carolina Piedmont, the Cherokee attacked the Hites with whom they had formerly been friends with little warning, dismembering Jacob Hite while alive and then throwing his torso into the house which they then burned down over his head. One of their sons, John, was also murdered by the Cherokee when he attempted to negotiate with them prior to the massacre, and Frances and two of her daughters were carried off as captive. Although Taverner Beale, Frances' son by her first marriage, had believed her to have ultimately survived and sought her ransom after the Revolution, the body of Frances Madison Beale Hite was said to have been recovered subsequently by the militia in the mountains of North Georgia and buried there; apparently, she had also been tortured before being murdered. The two daughters - Eleanor and Susan - were never found. George, oldest son of the Hites, had stayed in Virginia as a student at William and Mary and thus escaped the massacre. The marker is located on Gibbs Shoals Road (County Road 164) 0.1 miles north of East Suber Road (County Road 540), on the right when traveling south in Greenville County.

Figure 6

The Mannings were back in Hampshire County when Rev. Nathaniel Manning died early in 1777.[13] That year was a difficult one both for the country and for Mary. Washington's Army was barely surviving in miserable conditions at Valley Forge. Mary's Uncle Abraham had raised a Company of Hampshire Rangers[xix] and probably was there with him. Here was Mary, at age twenty-four, with two infant sons to care for, no husband and most of her close relatives living some distance away. Support for the Anglican Church

---

12   Courtesy of the Madison Family Organization.
13   Louise Willis in *Strictly a Family Affair* attributes this to a stroke since that is what killed his first cousin James Manning, president and founder of Brown University. It could have been anything.

was at a low ebb in Hampshire County.[14] Mary Manning had to move from The Glebe but where should she go? Her closest relatives were Abraham and Rebecca Hite at Fort Pleasant but Abraham was away and they were already talking about moving to Kentucky to be with their sons. We have good evidence that she then moved back to Berkeley County, where she had grown up.

Her husband's will, written in 1774, had made Mary his executrix and bequeathed to her the property given to him on Opequan Creek by her father. On February 11, 1777, Mary posted bond of 2,000 pounds in Hampshire County Court and was assisted in this by Abel Randall, a prosperous neighbor and church vestryman. A copy of the bond is shown in figure 7. The executors were Mary's uncle, Abraham Hite, and her older brother, Major Thomas Hite. Mary, evidently, then moved back to join her brother, Thomas, and his family.

---

14   Though it was not until later that Virginia declared the Anglican Church was not its official religion and financial support from the state was stopped.

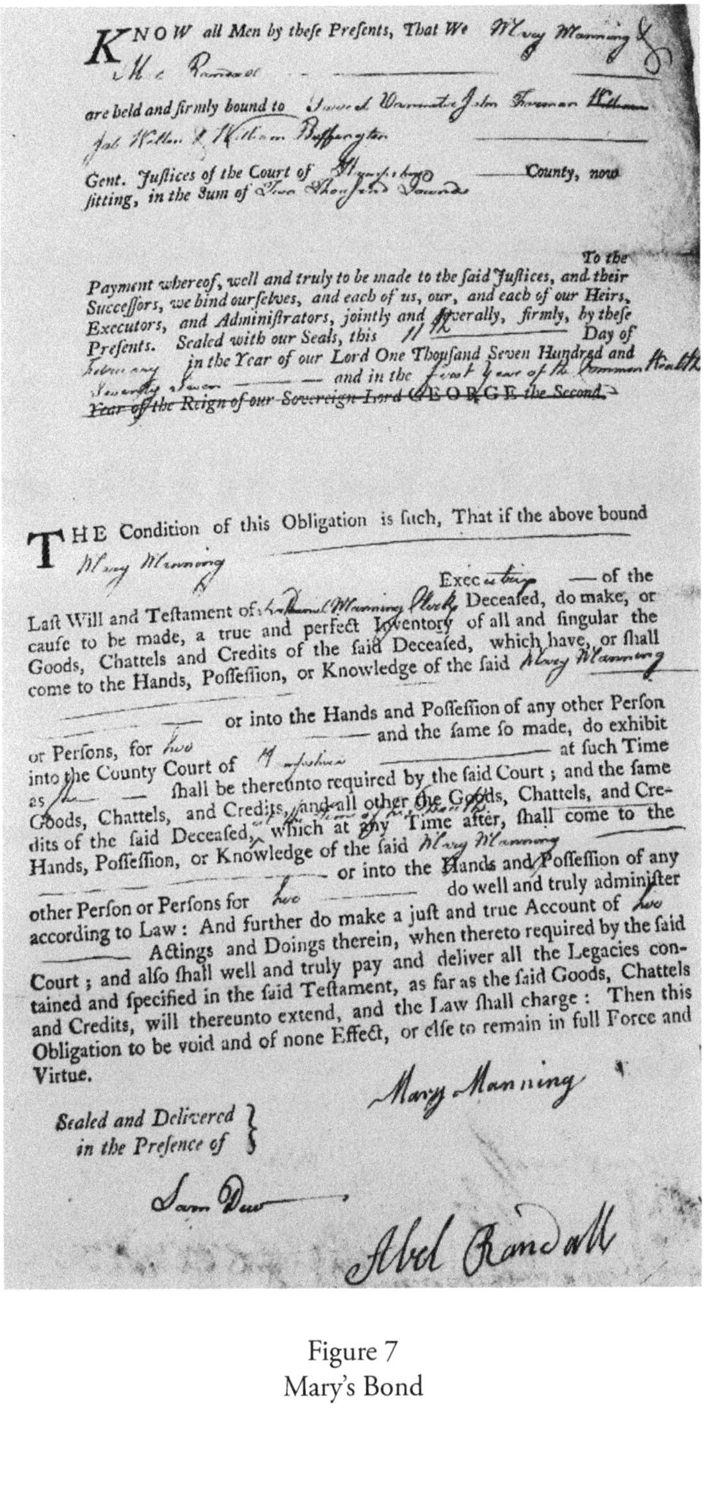

KNOW all Men by these Presents, That We *Mary Manning &*
Abel Randall

are held and firmly bound to *Samuel Warner & John Freeman William*
Jos. Willis & William Buffington

Gent. Justices of the Court of *Plymouth* ————— County, now
sitting, in the Sum of *Two Thousand Pounds*

                               To the
Payment whereof, well and truly to be made to the said Justices, and their
Successors, we bind ourselves, and each of us, our, and each of our Heirs,
Executors, and Administrators, jointly and severally, firmly, by these
Presents. Sealed with our Seals, this *11th* ————— Day of
February in the Year of our Lord One Thousand Seven Hundred and
Seventy Seven ————— and in the *first* Year of the *Commonwealth*
~~Year of the Reign of our Sovereign Lord GEORGE the Second.~~

THE Condition of this Obligation is such, That if the above bound
Mary Manning
                                    Exec *uting* ————— of the
Last Will and Testament of *Nathaniel Manning Clerk* Deceased, do make, or
cause to be made, a true and perfect Inventory of all and singular the
Goods, Chattels and Credits of the said Deceased, which have, or shall
come to the Hands, Possession, or Knowledge of the said *Mary Manning*

————————— or into the Hands and Possession of any other Person
or Persons, for *two* ————————— and the same so made, do exhibit
into the County Court of *Plymouth* ————————— at such Time
as ————— shall be thereunto required by the said Court; and the same
Goods, Chattels, and Credits, and all other the Goods, Chattels, and Credits of the said Deceased, which at any Time after, shall come to the
Hands, Possession, or Knowledge of the said *Mary Manning*
————————— or into the Hands and Possession of any
other Person or Persons for *two* ————————— do well and truly administer
according to Law: And further do make a just and true Account of *two*
————————— Actings and Doings therein, when thereto required by the said
Court; and also shall well and truly pay and deliver all the Legacies con-
tained and specified in the said Testament, as far as the said Goods, Chattels
and Credits, will thereunto extend, and the Law shall charge: Then this
Obligation to be void and of none Effect, or else to remain in full Force and
Virtue.

                                Mary Manning

Sealed and Delivered }
  in the Presence of }

Sam Dew

                        Abel Randall

Figure 7
Mary's Bond

1778–1787

Mary's Ten Years as a Widow

After marrying his stepsister in 1772, Thomas Hite had gotten involved solving his father's legal problems[xx] in Berkeley County and had founded his own estate, New Hopewell, on part of his father's property. When the war started, he volunteered and was wounded in the Battle of King's Bridge in 1775 and promoted to Major.[xxi] He then returned home and served in the Virginia General Assembly from 1776 through 1779.[xxii] He was the one who discovered his father's will and submitted it to the Berkeley Court in 1779. He was said to be a very proper individual and had a large library.

Thomas's own will was dated September 22, 1778. Contrary to some reports, he lived until shortly before August 17, 1779, when his will was proven in Berkeley County court.[xxiii] Mary Manning was a witness to both the will and the probate, along with her stepsister, Elizabeth Beale Harrison and Elizabeth's husband, George. This is good evidence that Mary had gone back home to Berkeley County and found refuge with her brother and stepsisters at New Hopewell. Both Mary and Frances were raising infant sons so they could come to each other's aid when things became desperate.

These years were difficult for all the women in the Hite families. Men of Mary's age were off fighting in the war and the

28

women had to run the estate. The slaves surely were helpful but were also a responsibility. Mary owned plenty of property but this, too, was a responsibility. In addition to the Opequan Creek property she had gotten from her husband, she was granted 1,000 acres of her father's land in South Carolina in 1784.[xxiv] You might say that she was land-poor but she did have wealthy cousins who ran horse and cattle ranches, planted crops, built flour mills and ran iron foundries.[xxv]

1777 had been the low point of the war. Washington had learned to dodge and baffle the British while waiting for France to provide help, which it eventually did. The war moved south and ended at Yorktown, Virginia, in October of 1781. The colonies struggled to get back to normalcy under the Articles of Confederation. The Treaty of Paris, ending the war officially and giving America land out to the Mississippi River, was finally signed in September 1783. America, however, was broke and only a series of French loans, negotiated by Franklin, were able to put her back on her feet. Settlers were moving westward into Kentucky and Ohio. Indian restlessness out there had not abated and the British, regardless of the treaty, were encouraging them.

Mary was too busy raising her kids to bother with these national issues, though she did follow the career of her stepcousin James Madison with great interest. After helping to write the Virginia constitution, he had now become a member of the Continental Congress.

As her sons grew more responsible, Mary was able to follow her social instincts and get around a bit. Based on her subsequent activities, it would appear that she was developing new interests. Her cousins, however, were still important to her. An elegant portrait of her cousin Major Isaac Hite Jr. is shown in figure 8. Long Meadows was now under his direction and he was developing it into a large and diverse family operation.[15] A graduate of William and Mary College where he reportedly received top honors,[16] he had married Nelly Conway Madison, the sister of James Madison.

---

15 Isaac Hite Jr. later started his own plantation nearby, a horse- and cattle-raising operation called Belle Grove. See the Hite papers at the Historical Society of Virginia.

16 Several sources say that he was the first college student elected to Phi Beta Kappa.

Figure 8
Cousin Isaac Hite Jr. by Charles Peale Polke

The marriage was held at Montpelier, the Madison homestead in Orange County, Virginia, in January of 1783. Mary would surely have attended their wedding, even in the middle of winter.

Her uncle John's estate and lodging house, Springdale (figure 1), lay ten miles to the north of Long Meadows and just five miles south of Winchester, which was becoming a small city.[17] There were also other relatives to visit. Her sister, Elizabeth Beale, and her cousins, the Bowmans and the Chrismans, lived just to the south of Long Meadows, in Shenandoah County where Mary's son, Nathaniel, had been born and baptized. Mary and her kids were certainly welcome to visit any of these relatives.

---

17   In the first census of 1840, it had 3454 residents. It now has about 25,000.

A REUNION IN MOOREFIELD

I n the summer of 1784, Mary took a trip out to Moorefield where she bought some property and met her uncle's family. The following is my interpretation of events but I believe it is a logical one.

In late June, Mary got a letter from Isaac Hite, Abraham's son, who had come back from Kentucky territory to see his parents at Fort Pleasant. Abraham Hite and Rebecca were now talking seriously about moving west to join their sons. Isaac and Abraham Jr. were worried that this might be a bit too much for them. They were just in their fifties but their lives had not been easy ones and they were showing their age. Abraham Hite had now reached the ripe old age of fifty-five and had been through a lot in his life. Rebecca was fifty.

"I wonder if you'd like to come out here and talk to them," wrote Isaac. "Moorefield has grown since you were here and I'm sure you'd like to see the place again. And we'd all like to see you and your kids. They must be growing like weeds."

This chance to show her sons, then eight and ten, where they used to live and meet their cousins really intrigued Mary. A chance to see Abe and Becky again and relive old memories but also what an opportunity for her sons to learn about the westward movement from men who knew the story firsthand. Early in July, she packed up the Hite family wagon, hitched up old Zeke and headed west to Fort Pleasant.

It was not an easy journey for Mary, having two rambunctious kids to cope with, but Mary took time to visit The Glebe and show her sons where they used to live. Lord Fairfax had died in 1781 and his will had left his Virginia properties to his nephew, Reverend Denny Martin of Kent, England.[18] Bill Heath and Bill Vance were still tenants farming the land around The Glebe and were anxious to show her the improvements they had made. It was a fun visit for Mary, knowing she could just look around and not have to worry about the condition of the house. Crossing the South Fork, the next day, was a bit of an adventure. The water level was low. That was not a problem but the kids kept rocking the wagon as they jumped from side to side looking up and down the river. Figure 9 is a view of The Trough looking north from where she forded the river.

Figure 9
South Fork of the Potomac Looking into The Trough

18   The title to the Fairfax lands was not resolved until 1816 in a famous case pitting the Virginia Supreme Court against the United States Supreme Court: *Martin v. Hunter's Lessee.*

The Early Records of Hampshire County say that on July 24, 1784, Mary Manning of Berkeley County bought Lot 17 in Moorefield from the Trustees of Hampshire County, part of a quantity of land being sold off in half-acre lots. On the same day, Isaac Hite of Lincoln County bought Lot Number 4.[xxvi] The record is clear, Isaac had moved west to Lincoln County in what is now the state of Kentucky but was then part of Virginia. Both transactions closed on August 10, 1784.

The documentation for these transactions answers one question but raises another. The wording of the deals confirms that Mary had indeed gone back to live in Berkeley County and that Isaac was then living in Kentucky territory. So why were she and Isaac buying property in Moorefield, which had been chartered only eight years ago? The terms of the sale required building a dwelling on the property. There is no evidence she ever did build, though she paid taxes in Hampshire County as late as 1789. Her property seems to have eventually become the site of the present Hardy County Courthouse,[xxvii] shown in figure 10.

Isaac Hite had been exploring out in Kentucky County since 1773. In a letter written to his father from Kentucky on April 26, 1783, Isaac described in some detail the properties out there that his father was interested in buying.[xxviii] So why did Isaac Hite buy a half-acre property in Moorefield in August 1784 when he was already living in Kentucky and his father was considering the move himself?

About six weeks later, on September 27, 1784, General George Washington, on the way back from a trip to Ohio, stayed with Colonel Abraham Hite at his home at Fort Pleasant. Washington wrote about this in his diary.[xxix] He rested there on the twenty-eighth, discussing navigation on the Potomac[19] with Colonel Hite and Colonel Joseph Neville. He left the next day for Rockingham taking Captain Hite, the colonel's son, with him to show the way. The stories that were later told about this trip all concluded that

---

19   Washington was intrigued with the idea of a navigable water passage to the Ohio and Mississippi rivers. He must certainly have known of Isaac Hite's exploration s back there in 1774 (see earlier footnote.)

this was Captain Abraham Hite Jr. and this is probably correct. Young Abraham wrote to General Washington from Kentucky four months later, in January of 1785,[xxx] to respond to questions raised by Washington—probably on this trip. If so, that puts both of Hite's sons and Mary in Moorefield and Fort Pleasant in August and September of 1784.

Mary and the Hite boys were surely having a family conference, asking the senior Hites to stay in Moorefield and assuring them that they would still have family around—"Look at those properties we just bought in Moorefield."

This did not work. The Abraham Hites moved on to Kentucky anyway.[xxxi] Abraham Sr. died in Louisville in 1790 and Isaac died there in 1794. Abraham Jr. had also moved to Kentucky and lived there until his death in 1832.

Figure 10
Hardy County Courthouse

MARY MANNING, SCHOOLTEACHER

The country was now getting back to normal after the war and things were finally looking up for Mary Manning. Her sons were growing up and she needed to look after their schooling. A number of her Hite cousins had gone to college. Mary was not in a position to do that for her sons but they needed a good basic education. So what did she do? Mary started her own boarding school and taught her brother John's three daughters along with her own two sons. The youngest Hite girl was the same age as Mary's son, Nathaniel. Mary Manning was a lady of many talents and good textbooks could be found in her brother Thomas's library.[xxxii]

Mary's brother John, like her husband Nathaniel, had died early in 1777.[20] His wife, Sarah, had remarried—this time to a Winchester lawyer named Alexander White—and they became the guardians of three Hite daughters named Catherine, Mary and Sarah. Their orphan guardianship papers show that for three years, from 1785 through 1787, Mary Manning was being paid for schooling and board for these three orphans.[xxxiii] The papers for Sarah are shown as figure 11. Evidence exists to show that Mary's school was in Berkeley County—one item for expense shows a local trip to nearby Shepherdstown for supplies. There are also several

---

20   John Hite's will was dated October 25, 1776, and the will was proven on March 18, 1777.

trips to Alexandria that are paid for but no direct evidence that Mary was involved.

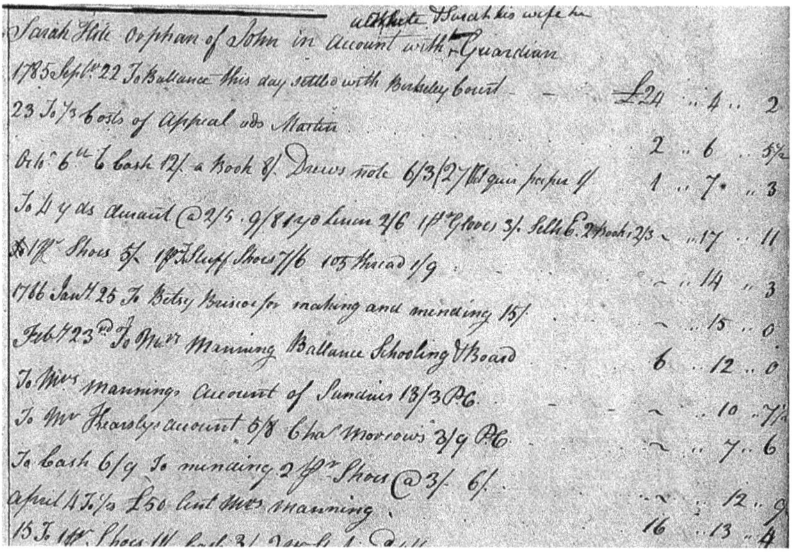

Figure 11
School and Board for Sarah Hite from her Orphan Papers

Mary must have done a good job with these girls. Their stepfather, Alexander White (1738–1804), educated in Scotland, was a well-known lawyer in Winchester. He had taken over Abraham Hite's seat in the Virginia House of Burgesses in 1772. He served in the US House of Representatives from 1789 to 1793 and was writing frequently to James Madison during that period. A letter of his dated Woodville, February 17, 1794, tells how the Hite girls had grown up and married.[xxxiv] Catherine (Nelly) had married Theodorick Lee, brother of Light Horse Harry Lee, and Sarah (Sally) had married Alexander Pitt Buchanan of Baltimore. Mary (Polly) had yet to be married but later references indicate that she married twice, the second time to Jonathan Guest of St. Louis.[xxxv] These girls were well taken care of by their stepfather and Mary Manning's teaching had obviously been effective.

The known attendance at Mary's school is limited to the three nieces but her own two sons were of school age and so were her stepsister's children. It is only a guess but she may well have been teaching at New Hopewell, living with her deceased brother Thomas's family and using his excellent library. If so, there is a parallel today. New Hopewell is currently (in 2019) the New Hopewell Center for the Arts and includes the dance studio shown in figure 12.

Figure 12
New Hopewell Dance Studio

MARY'S SECOND MARRIAGE

Mary was now getting restless and looking for a change in life. We really have no idea how she met William Bushby, a house painter and widower who lived in Alexandria, and we probably won't ever know unless a personal diary shows up. But it is interesting to speculate.

Alexandria was the closest open water port to Berkeley County and Jacob Hite had owned several properties there, down near the waterfront. The trip to Alexandria might well have been one of Mary's cherished memories from her childhood. But that was long ago.

William Bushby owned property down near those Hite properties. Perhaps that's where they met but there seems no good reason for Mary to have gone to Alexandria in the 1780s. Perhaps she did so just for old time's sake or to make some purchases for her boarding school. There also seems no good reason for William Bushby to visit Mary's area of Virginia unless, perhaps, he got a house painting job in Winchester. He had painted George Washington's house near Alexandria in 1770. Winchester was Washington's old stamping ground and who knows, perhaps George had recommended Bushby to a friend who lived there. Winchester was right in the heart of Hite family territory. There is no record of this happening but it does seem possible that they met in this manner.

But even if they met this way, what drew them together? I have to think that it was religion. That's how people commonly met their future wives and husbands in those days. William Bushby had been one of the earliest converts to Methodism before he ever came to America[xxxvi] and continued to play a prominent role in Methodist affairs until he died. Mary did not come from an overly religious family but after all, she had married an Anglican minister and some of her Hite cousins had adopted the Methodist religion. John Hite Jr. and his sister had become committed Methodists and they built a Methodist Church at Stephensburg (now Stephens City) near Winchester some time before 1788. John's sister then married a man named Phelps, who became a Methodist minister.[xxxvii] There is also an indication that a Van Meter, out in Hardy County, had become a Methodist and released his slaves.

All were very familiar with the name Francis Asbury (figure 13). He was an itinerant Anglican preacher who had been sent over to America in 1771, by John Wesley,[21] to preach Methodism. Nathaniel Manning was in England being ordained at that time and would certainly have known of Asbury's assignment.

Figure 13
Francis Asbury

---

21 Wesley was an Anglican minister who, while a graduate student at Oxford in 1729, had taken a different, more personal approach to the Anglican religion. He and his brother, Charles, were branded as Methodist by students at Oxford who laughed at the methodical way they ordered their lives.

Asbury visited the Martinsburg/Winchester/South Branch area in Virginia in the late spring and early summer every year from 1781 through 1786, staying with John Hite while preaching in Winchester and at Richard William's house when out on the South Branch.[xxxviii] In July 1783, Asbury presided at a funeral at Isaac Hite's residence, Long Meadows.

Mary would have wanted to see what Asbury was up to, especially since he was staying at her uncle's lodge. William Bushby would not have missed a chance to hear Asbury preach if he was in the area. That could possibly explain how Mary met her second husband and was attracted to him. The following is a depiction of how they might have met and found some common interests.

* * * * *

It was a Sunday in June in 1786 and Francis Asbury was preaching to a crowd of two hundred people on the grounds of Springfield, John Hite's hostelry south of Winchester. The crowd was a bit unruly. In Asbury's own words, "A difficult group. Religion is greatly wanting in these parts. The inhabitants are much divided; made up, as they are, of different nations, and speaking different languages, they agree in scarcely anything, except it be to sin against God."

The room was warm and it was obvious that William Bushby was perturbed. He kept mopping his brow with a handkerchief and was whisking away at a buzzing fly when he heard a pleasant female voice say, "Care for a cool glass of water? You look a bit uncomfortable."

He looked up at a pretty young woman, about thirty years of age, who was carrying a pitcher of water.

"Why, yes, thank you." He looked at her questioningly.

"I'm Mary Manning, John Hite's niece. I hope you're enjoying yourself."

"Well, I am a bit nervous. I'm worried for Mr. Asbury. Of course, he's used to this sort of thing."

"I know what you mean. My husband was a preacher too."

"Was?"

"Oh, yes. It was too much for him. He died five years ago out in Hampshire County."

That peaked William's interest and he asked her to explain. Then it all came tumbling out—the years trying to be a good minister's wife with her husband off tending to his far-flung parish much of the time. William then introduced himself to her and told of his long interest in Methodism, which had just separated from the Anglican Church and elected Francis Asbury and Thomas Coke as bishops.

When he asked Mary to a Methodist Church social event,[22] she accepted and they had a great time. They started seeing each other regularly and she found him friendly and amusing. One thing they discussed avidly was slavery since the Methodist society was then recommending setting all slaves free. Only a year ago, William had entertained Asbury and Coke at his house in Alexandria where they talked about eliminating slavery.[xxxix]

William had a number of female slaves and most of them had children. Mary had lived with slaves all her life; they were like part of her family. Raising young children without a husband, negro slaves had become indispensable. Yet they both could see the injustice of slavery, as his church was forcefully pointing out.

"I'd free all of them all right now if I thought they could fend for themselves," William declared.

"Then you need to judge each individual case," said Mary. "Free them when you think they can handle the responsibility."

It was not long before he asked her to marry him. That was quite a decision for her to make. She would be moving away from family and friends and basically giving away her inherited fortune. What would her relatives think? Mary was attracted to Bushby, his ideas and his dedication to them. Her sons were now entering onto their teens and a father would be a big help. So when William Bushby asked her to marry him, she accepted readily—this time for love.

Mary realized that William Bushby's viewpoint on slavery was a sharp break from her past and that it might alienate her wealthy

---

22 Asbury refers to these as love-feasts.

Hite relatives. Thinking it over, however, she felt that honest labor as a painter was more worthy than being dependent on a lot of unfortunate slaves for one's livelihood.

* * * * *

The Hites might well have objected to her marriage but were too distracted to bother. They were more concerned about Nelly's brother, James Madison. He seemed to them to be getting in over his head in politics.

James Madison was concerned about governance in the thirteen states, which seemed to him to be drifting aimlessly under the Articles of Confederation with the several states not cooperating with each other. He was convinced that a Union of States was necessary, though he knew there would be strenuous objections. Others thought that some simple amendments to the Articles were all that was necessary. The country was evenly divided on the matter.[xl]

James Madison had written Virginia's constitution and had ideas for a new United States constitution—setting up a bicameral legislature, a presidency. and a judiciary with equal powers—and George Washington agreed with him. Twisting Washington's arm, he got him to chair a Constitutional Convention in 1787. It was Madison who drafted the Constitution, debated Patrick Henry on the issues, made modifications and eventually got it ratified in the summer of 1788. A small fellow with big ideas, Mary's stepcousin James Madison became one of our founding fathers.[xli]

1789–1810

Raising Another Family

Mary Manning and William Bushby were married sometime after 1787 and before 1789 (one source says February 5, 1788) and she and her sons moved in to live with him. He owned a substantial brick house in Alexandria with four rooms and a front portico plus a one-acre fenced-in garden with fruit trees, all with the necessary outbuildings. He was a widower with two grown children and had a cousin named Nancy living with him. Over the next two years, William freed all his slaves. In all, he freed eleven slaves: four negro women over nineteen years old and seven children under the age of thirteen, three boys and four girls. The term of their freedom ranged from immediate to twenty-four years (for an infant). He gave them their freedom after the period that he deemed necessary for each of them to find their way as freemen.[xlii] They must have lived in some of those outbuildings, run the farm and did chores.

You do have to wonder how all this worked. Sarah, the oldest slave, was thirty-five and was freed immediately in 1879. She may have wanted to stay, watch over her own children and serve the Bushbys as a free personal servant but Virginia's slavery laws were very restrictive and she may well have moved elsewhere. Mary, age twenty-five, was freed in 1890 but Milly, age twenty-seven, was not freed until 1795. Perhaps Molly, age one, was her child and needed her mother. At any rate, there were enough of them still around, slave or freemen, to help with the farm and household chores. Cousin Nancy, of course, was the main help when new Bushby children came along.

They soon had three daughters: Eliza Hite Bushby, born in 1790; Catherine Bruce Bushby, born in 1792; and Mary Hite Bushby, born in 1795. Jacob and Nathaniel Manning, now in their twenties, lived with the Bushby family for a time but they valued their Hite family connections and were often off visiting people out in western Virginia.

Many changes had occurred in the United States under the presidency of George Washington, who served from 1789 to 1797. Among these was the selection, in 1790, of the District of Columbia, at the confluence of the Potomac and Anacostia Rivers, as the new site of the nation's capital, to be occupied by the year 1800. This was only a few miles north and across the Potomac River from where the Bushbys lived. White House construction was started in 1792 and President John Adams moved in to the unfinished building in 1800, as planned. The story of how this all came to be is both interesting in itself and pertinent to later developments in the Bushby family history so let's digress for a moment.

WASHINGTON, DC, IN THE EARLY 1800S

The selection of Washington, DC, as our national capital was largely influenced by prominent Roman Catholics, men such as Charles Carroll of Carrolton, a signer of the Declaration of Independence and a member of the Constitutional Convention. The Capitol Hill area on which the city was built was the property of his cousin, Daniel Carroll of Duddington, who played a key role in President Washington's selection of the site and Notley Young, who owned part of Duddington Pasture. The capital city became a focal point for Catholics, a place where they were on equal footing with their neighbors. Many were elected to public office and US presidents made a point of attending local Catholic services on special occasions.[23] Early Washington, DC, and particularly the Georgetown area, appears to have been a place where Catholics found themselves accepted on their merits.

All this was a far cry from the situation as recently as 1755 when Catholics in Maryland and Virginia were asked to pay double taxes because they were not serving in the military even though the law stated they could not join the military. For over a hundred years, Catholics in Maryland had been a minority, subject to a variety

---

23   Much of this description owes a debt to William W. Warner's book, *At Peace with All Their Neighbors: Catholics and Catholicism in the National Capital 1776–1860*, Georgetown University Press, Washington, DC, 1994.

of laws forbidding them to hold public office, worship publicly or establish Catholic schools. Catholics, however, participated fully in the Revolutionary War, General Henry Carbery being an excellent example. The Catholic situation changed dramatically with the Declaration of Independence and the Religious Freedom Amendment to the Constitution. American Catholics welcomed a government that not only protected freedom of religion but also protected freedom from religion.

Catholics in St. Mary's County had adapted to their former situation by trying not to flaunt their faith. They got along and many prospered. Some of them were, in fact, the largest land owners in the state. They sent their sons abroad to be educated in their religion and a number of them became priests but all this was done privately. When the national capital welcomed them, these Catholics knew how to get along with their Protestant neighbors. A number of them moved to Georgetown, a preexisting shipping port on the fall line of the Potomac River that had already established a Catholic church and Catholic schools before the national capital even existed.[24]

Archbishop John Carroll, a cousin of Charles and Daniel Carroll, came to America at a very opportune moment, in 1774, and set about to develop churches, schools and a home-grown priesthood. He was largely successful. Based in Philadelphia, where the Quakers had long practiced religious freedom, Carroll nevertheless recognized Washington, DC, as his main opportunity. He established Georgetown College in 1789 as the nation's first Catholic and Jesuit University. Archbishop Leonard Neale (figure 14), one of its first presidents, then founded Visitation Convent in Georgetown in 1794 and Visitation Academy for women opened in 1799, the year before John Adams moved into the unfinished White House.

---

24 Georgetown was also the terminus of George Washington's proposed shipping route to the Mississippi River via the Potomac and Ohio Rivers.

Figure 14
Archbishop Leonard Neale

Figure 15
Washington, DC, in 1834

THE MOVE TO WASHINGTON

M ary's life span covered the period of early industrial development in America. The United States was beginning slowly to enter into its own Industrial Revolution. Ben Franklin did his kite experiment in 1752. The first steam engine in America was used in 1755 to pump water from a mine. In 1787, John Fitch tried out a forty-five-foot steamboat on the Delaware River and by 1800, Oliver Evans was predicting construction of a railway between New York and Washington, a feat that would not come to pass until 1834. As part of the new government, a United States Navy Department was organized and in 1799, land for the Washington, DC, Navy Yard was set aside, only a short distance up the Anacostia River from where it emptied into the Potomac. Figure 15 shows Washington in 1834 with the Anacostia River in the foreground.

All this created a need for skilled workers. William Bushby sold his house in Alexandria in 1800 and moved to the city, to be where the work was. Figure 16 is a copy of his 1799 advertisement to sell his properties. Originally, he picked Georgetown but then got the main painting assignment at the Navy Yard and purchased a house near there, presumably the one on M Street between Tenth and Eleventh that is referred to in his will.

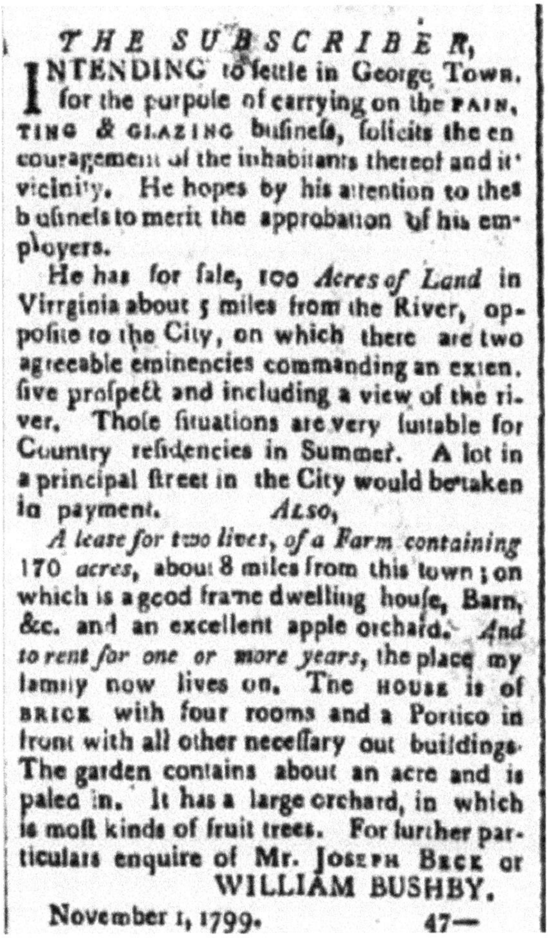

THE SUBSCRIBER, INTENDING to settle in George Town, for the purpose of carrying on the PAINTING & GLAZING business, solicits the encouragement of the inhabitants thereof and it' vicinity. He hopes by his attention to the business to merit the approbation of his employers.

He has for sale, 100 *Acres of Land* in Virginia about 5 miles from the River, opposite to the City, on which there are two agreeable eminencies commanding an extensive prospect and including a view of the river. Those situations are very suitable for Country residencies in Summer. A lot in a principal street in the City would be taken in payment. *ALSO,*

A lease for two lives, of a Farm containing 170 *acres,* about 8 miles from this town; on which is a good frame dwelling house, Barn, &c. and an excellent apple orchard. *And to rent for one or more years,* the place my family now lives on. The HOUSE is of BRICK with four rooms and a Portico in front with all other necessary out buildings. The garden contains about an acre and is paled in. It has a large orchard, in which is most kinds of fruit trees. For further particulars enquire of Mr. JOSEPH BECK or
WILLIAM BUSHBY.
November 1, 1799.   47—

Figure 16
William Bushby Sells His House

Mary did not openly promote her connections with James Madison but did allow others to make contacts for her. Her husband's job at the Navy Yard had been helped by a discreet intervention from her half-brother, George Hite, and Bushby followed up on this with a personal letter to George's first cousin James Madison, in 1805, trying to secure his position there from threatened competition.[xliii] Madison, then Secretary of State, was happy to oblige and William got the assignment.

George Hite wrote to James Madison a number of other times.[25] In 1806, he asked Madison for advice in recovering some slaves captured by the Cherokee Nation when they killed his father. Cartmell[xliv] tells how George was able to recover one black girl and learn of the fate of his sister Eleanor, who had been rescued and wooed by a British officer named Johnson but died shortly thereafter in Pensacola.

In 1809, George wrote Madison again, this time looking for civil positions for his sons, Jacob and Robert. He worded this letter very slyly, "From the connection which exists between Mr. Madison and myself, I am deterred from making any personal application to him lest he suppose that I was presuming upon that connection." Then he goes ahead and recommends Robert to a position as a private secretary asking Madison for any assistance he can give.[xlv] George Hite was named first clerk of Court in Jefferson County when it was established in 1801 and his son Robert took over the job after George died.

---

25 Alexander White was also a prolific correspondent. Twenty-two of his letters are found in the James Madison papers, mostly concerning politics.

GEORGE HITE'S INHERITANCE

George was now Mary's last surviving brother, actually her half-brother. He was the only Hite relative that she continued to contact regularly after marrying William Bushby and as we have just seen, he had been helpful to William. When their father died in 1776, his will was not found for three more years. Shortly after his half-brother found it, Thomas Hite died and George became the last male survivor. But he was not mentioned in the will. His half-brother John had assumed he had inherited his father's property when he wrote his own will in October 1776 and a legal battle ensued. Fourteen years later, George Hite was forced to sue the three daughters of John Hite in order to obtain his patrimony. This is mentioned in a letter George wrote to James Madison in 1790[xlvi] asking him to deliver some legal documents to Alexander White, the guardian of John's children. From the tone of the letter, it sounds like George considered White, a lawyer, as a definite obstacle to his case.

Mary Bushby was sympathetic and thought George had a right to his inheritance. She became party to a 1793 petition signed by Jacob Hite's other descendants who wanted litigation to stop and George to be provided for and in 1794, this was accomplished. George is then awarded all claims to land owned by Jacob Hite in 1770 except for one-fifths of lands to be recovered from Lord Fairfax's estate, one-fifths of the profits from Rising Sun

Mine in Rockingham County and 1,000 acres of land in South Carolina. George became administrator of his father's will, assumed responsibility for all debts of Jacob Hite and released claims against the estate of John Hite.[xlvii]

In an 1804 court case, George is named as the administrator of his father's will. The plaintiff had gotten a judgment against Jacob Hite before the Revolution which had not been satisfied when the will was settled. Named as defendants were the descendants of John Hite and Thomas Hite as well as Mary Hite and William Bushby.[xlviii]

THE BUSHBYS'
NEW FRIENDS

———————

Mary and her three daughters adapted well to life in the capital. Washington itself was sparsely settled as seen previously in figure 15, a depiction of the city in 1834, a quarter century later. Where they lived, however, good neighbors were all around and good schools were available. The Bushby family soon developed new interests and a whole new circle of friends.

The Navy Yard provided most of these new contacts and prominent among these were the Catholic Carbery family. Thomas Carbery Sr. was a contractor/builder in St. Mary's County who supplied much of the heavy lumber used in constructing the White House,[xlix] bringing it in via his wharf on Tiber Creek. When he was offered the job of lumber inspector at the new Washington Navy Yard by Secretary of the Navy Stafford, he accepted and moved his large Catholic family from St. Mary's County to Georgetown in 1805. Since both men were working on construction projects at the Navy Yard, the Bushby and Carbery families got know each other well.

The Carbery children all became solid citizens of Washington, DC, playing important roles and achieving a degree of notoriety. Martha was married to Salvadore Catalana, an officer in the new US Navy who had been a ship's pilot with Admiral Decatur at Tripoli in 1804. Joseph was a Jesuit priest at St. Inigoes church in St. Mary's County. Thomas, shown in figure 17, was an army captain in the war of 1812. He later became a bank president and was mayor of

Washington from 1822 to 1824. James is listed in as an apprentice to his father at the Navy Yard in 1808. He then trained briefly as a naval architect but became involved in city politics, becoming a city councilman in the 1830s and, finally, a judge. Lewis was a civil engineer and is remembered as the Surveyor of the County of Washington.[1] Ruth and Catherine had remained spinsters and were living with Thomas.

Figure 17
Mayor Thomas Carbery

But daughter Ann Carbery was a special situation. Born in 1784 and married to John Mattingly in 1803, their marriage fell apart and she had moved in with her brother Thomas in 1815 with her two children. She contracted abdominal cancer and was bedridden by

1819. In the summer of 2011, a long-awaited book was published called *Mrs. Mattingly's Miracle: The Prince, the Widow and the Cure that Shocked Washington City*. The author, Nancy Lusignan Schultz, is professor of English at Salem State College in Massachusetts. The centerpiece of the story is the sudden and complete cure of Ann Carbery Mattingly from a horrendously debilitating cancerous tumor. This actually occurred at Mayor Thomas Carbery's mansion, shown in figure 18. Immediately upon receiving communion at 4 in the morning of March 10, 1824, apparently as a direct result of special prayers recommended by a charismatic Austrian priest, Prince Hohenlohe, Ann Mattingly rose and, thanking God, declared herself cured. A number of witnesses were present, including Anne Maria Fitzgerald (a close family friend), several of Ann's sisters, her brother Lewis and her daughter Susan. The event was exhaustively studied and testimony taken from all who were present. An 1830 report by the Bishop of Charleston to the Bishop of Baltimore examined all the evidence, citing the testimony of witnesses.

Figure 18
Thomas Carbery's Mansion: Corner 17th and C

Ann Mattingly then went over to the Visitation Convent and tried to join the sisters. They took her in but decided she was not destined to become a nun. The whole episode is told in *A Story of Courage: Annals of the Georgetown Convent of the Visitation of the Blessed Virgin Mary* by George Parsons Lathrop and Rose Hawthorne Lathrop, [26] Riverside Press, Cambridge, 1895.

Schultz dwells at length on the negative reaction to the miracle by religious communities in a nation that was still learning how to handle religious freedom. Basically, they ridiculed or tried to play down any interpretation of this as a true miracle. And this included the Catholic bishops who did not want to cause trouble. On the other hand, Nancy Schultz does not mention the numerous conversions to Catholicism that occurred as a result of the miracle.

We know that William Bushby had remained a staunch Methodist, having helped establish the Methodist Church in the Alexandria area and Mary had often entertained visiting Methodist ministers. He was well aware of that fact that Georgetown was full of Catholics when he moved there. St. Mary's Catholic Church in Alexandria had been a mission church of Trinity Parish in Georgetown and after the Bushbys moved to Georgetown, Pastor Neale of Trinity Church purchased the former Methodist meeting house in Alexandria as a site for a permanent St. Mary's parish.

---

26   Rose was Nathaniel Hawthorne's sister.

THE MANNING BOYS

B ack in 1798, Mary's son Jacob Hite Manning (shown on the front cover of *Growing with America: Colonial Roots*) had married a rich widow named Mary (Polly) Rutherford (nee Darke) (1772–1843) who was from Jefferson County, Virginia. They lived on an estate called Woodlawn in Charles Town, Virginia, (now West Virginia) not far from Leetown, where Mary had grown up. About sixty miles northeast of Washington, DC, Woodlawn can be reached today in about eighty-five minutes but with several river crossings, it was an overnight trip in those days.[li] Several Manning grandchildren were born in the early 1800s, one of whom, another Nathaniel, is shown in figure 19. A family history book, *The Descendants of the Rev. Nathaniel Manning, MD: Strictly a Family Affair*, by Louise Edrington Willis, privately published in March 1953, provides further information on the Jacob Hite Manning family and their descendants. The author has completely missed the fact that Mary had another son; Nathaniel, Junior.

Figure 19
Nathaniel Manning, Mary's grandson

Mary's younger son, Nathaniel Manning Jr., moved with the Bushbys to Georgetown but had developed business interests in nearby Loudoun County, Virginia, where he became involved with David Lacey, a rather relaxed Quaker farmer, in some real estate transactions. He married David and Sarah Lacey's youngest daughter, Euphemia Lacy[27] in Leesburg, Virginia, in 1803. Between 1810 and 1820, Nathaniel was a Presbyterian Church trustee in Waterford and an appraiser and seller of estates and slaves. He was reported as selling lots and a tavern in Waterford.[lii] He may also have been involved in setting up a bank there. By 1820, they had given Mary seven granddaughters, most of whom appear to have attended the Visitation Academy in Georgetown.[liii] This was part of the Visitation Convent, shown in figure 20 as it existed a half century later.

---

27 Euphemia, Diademia, Thurza and Castelina Lacy were the daughters of David Lacy and Sarah Pancoast.

Figure 20
Visitation Convent in 1895

Somewhere along the line, David Lacey had bought 600-plus acres of prime farm and woodland, lying halfway between Waterford and Leesburg and started a tavern at what is now the intersection of routes 662 and 7.[liv] A natural spring gave abundant fresh water year round and he undoubtedly used this as a mixer. Known as Twin Elms, this is where Euphemia was born and it became the property of Euphemia and her husband Nathaniel Manning after David Lacey died in 1818. Euphemia describes this land as her farm in her 1859 will. They were living there in 1828 when their only son, another Jacob Hite Manning, was born. Nathaniel Manning died in 1830.

Leesburg is about forty miles, as the crow flies, from downtown Washington and about twenty miles from where Nathaniel's brother lived. There were rivers to cross but this was close enough for holiday get-togethers. Mary Hite Manning Bushby was extremely pleased when Euphemia and Nathaniel named their first daughter after her. Mary Hite Manning was born near Leesburg in 1805. Euphemia and her daughters all ended up living in Washington. The Bushby and Carbery family connections appear to be the reason.

WILLIAM BUSHBY DIES AS MADISON TAKES OVER FROM JEFFERSON

America's relationship with Britain was tense during the early 1800s. The Napoleonic Wars were raging between Britain and France and they had resulted in Britain's imposing economic sanctions on America and impressing American sailors. When Jefferson was reelected in 1804, he was under pressure to do something and eventually started an embargo on British goods which actually hurt Americans more than the British. American anger came to a head when the USS *Chesapeake* was attacked and boarded by HMS *Leopard* off Norfolk in 1807. Hotheads like Henry Clay were predicting war. In 1812, with Madison in office, Congress declared war against the British.

Nevertheless, things went along smoothly for Mary and her family during Jefferson's term of office. She had important connections in the administration but was reluctant to use them.[lv] James Madison, the Secretary of State, was still a reserved "little old man," but his wife, Dolley, compensated for that with her warmth and party spirit. But just as Jefferson's term of office expired and Madison took over as president in 1809, William Bushby became ill, possibly from the consequences of painting with the lead-based paints of that era. He died in July of 1810 and Mary again was left with fatherless children and not much money. This time, however, there were three capable and attractive young ladies, fifteen, eighteen and twenty years old who could help with household chores.

In his will, William Bushby had written:

"In consideration of that confidence which my much loved wife placed in me at our marriage, by taking my word for the use and distribution of all her property then put in my power, the aforesaid of which that I have applied to my own purposes, I do not think will be more after any debts are paid than will replace that estate which she possessed when she was married. And that I have known her faithful conduct for more than twenty years have therefore sufficient reason to place my entire confidence in her respecting the use and application of any estate that I may be in possession of at the time of my decease. I therefore give and desire to my faithful wife, Mary Bushby and ordain her the sole executrix of this my last will and testament. All my real and personal property, whether of lands, moneys, goods, etc. to her and to her heirs and assigns for ever to be applied by her agreeable to her own judgment."

He was right; it turns out that William Bushby left Mary, now fifty-six years old, a lot of mortgaged property and a sea of debts, though he, himself, had an unpaid claim on George Washington for having painted his yacht. Mary was in a difficult position financially and had to do something.

1810–1814

The Boarding House

Even before her husband's death, Mary decided to start a boarding house in Washington with the help of her daughters. The will states that they were then living at a house they owned south of Capitol Hill and north of the Navy Yard on M Street between Tenth and Eleventh, certainly a good location for a boarding house. The boarding house itself, however, appears to have been rented property on Capitol Hill.

There were a number of such houses in Washington, catering to new members of Congress. They had some important men living there. One of their boarders was James Carbery who was then assisting his father at the Navy Yard.

The War of 1812 was imminent and the Bushby girls heard some interesting debates going on. The men called it the war mess at Mrs. Dawson's in 1811 but the next year, they were all at Mary Bushby's. John C. Calhoun (figure 21), the newly elected Representative from South Carolina, had decided as early as 1807 that war with Britain was inevitable. Calhoun returned home to Mrs. Bushby's Boarding House in November 1812 and suggested an idea to his fellow boarder, Captain Stewart, "of putting Congress in a better humor with the Navy." Henry Clay, a tall, fiery, young Kentuckian, who was then Speaker of the House, was also living there. According to a recent (2014) book about Henry Clay,[lvi] they all held a meeting at Mary's boardinghouse that became famous. They discussed the poor condition of the American Navy and Stewart brought with him Lieutenant Ridgely, his confidential officer and first Lieutenant of the frigate *Constitution*. Convinced that war with Britain was inevitable, the topic was how to get the public more involved. Stewart then arranged a sumptuous all-day reception aboard the USS *Constitution* for Thursday, November 26, Thanksgiving Day. Everyone went including President Madison and his wife, Dolley. All the Bushby women were there and they had congressional escorts.

Figure 21
John C. Calhoun

Stewart, in 1861, just before the Civil War, wrote a remarkable letter that describes his own version of the 1812 meeting and his reading of Calhoun[28] as a devoted Southern States Rights advocate. He remembered it a little differently:

---

28   Calhoun later became US vice president under John Quincy Adams and Andrew Jackson.

"Letter from Commodore Stewart. My Dear Sir: Bordentown, May, 4, 1861. Agreeably to your request I now furnish you with the reminiscences of a conversation which passed between Mr. John C. Calhoun and myself, in the latter part of December, 1812, after the declaration of war by the Congress of the United States against Great Britain, on the 18th of June previous. On the assembling of Congress, in the early part of December, I found that an important portion of the leading Democratic members of Congress had taken up their quarters at Mrs. Bushby's boarding-house; amongst whom was Mr. Calhoun—a new member from South Carolina—and I believe this was his first appearance in the House of Representatives. In consequence of this I took Lieutenant Ridgley, my confidential officer and the first Lieutenant of the frigate *Constellation*, of which vessel I then held the command, and was preparing for sea at the Washington navy yard—left our lodgings at Strothers' and obtained board at Mrs. Bushby's with them. Ridgley was a witty and able talker, who could aid me in demonstrating the necessity for, and the high policy of a formidable naval force, wherewith to carry on the war with England, which I considered could only be done with effect through her being victoriously struck at on an element over which she deemed herself sole mistress. This appeared to me to constitute her most tender point. By this movement I found myself judiciously located to enable me to urge upon Congress any patriotic measures which seemed best calculated to meet and discomfit the self-sufficiency and arrogance of our oppressive enemy."

This was impressive company for Mary and her daughters and they got a first-hand education in what was going on in congress. But things could get difficult sometimes. While her mother supervised the kitchen, Eliza waited on the table and found it quite a challenge. Some of the boarders were quite offensive, particularly when they had too much to drink or tried to get too personal. Senator Richard Brent of Virginia was a heavy drinker and William Sanford was trying to woo her, until he died during the 1813 congressional session.

A more respectable boarder was Quaker Congressman (and later Senator) Jonathan Roberts, an ardent Madison supporter. He has left us an informative set of memoirs written to his daughter.[lvii] According to Roberts, this was a large rented house where Mary Bushby, in turn, rented rooms to as many as twelve boarders. With her connections, Mary was able to attract a well-heeled clientele of government employees. Roberts had his doubts about the safety of the room heaters but kept coming back and part of the reason was Eliza. A portrait of Roberts is shown in figure 22.

Figure 22
Johnathan Roberts
Oil on Wood
Library of Congress Prints and Photographs
Division Washington, DC

In 1812, Mary's second daughter, Catherine, married a Methodist minister, later a bishop, named Beverly Waugh and they moved to Clarksburg, Maryland, about thirty miles away—a relatively easy trip for a visit. The war of 1812 was now underway but Mary and her two other daughters (Eliza, twenty-two, and Mary, seventeen) continued to run the boarding house as we have already seen.

Jonathan Roberts boarded with Mary during the summer of 1813 and quickly became enamored with Eliza. She "presided at the dining table, was attractive and well mannered." When the congressional session was over and as he was preparing to go home to Norristown, Pennsylvania, Eliza gives him a letter to take to her sister, Catherine Waugh, in Baltimore. She is not there so he writes Eliza a letter, which she acknowledges and he responds carefully but warmly. When he comes back for the fall term, he cautiously asks for her hand in marriage, pointing out that he would soon become a senator.

Her mother was delighted to agree and with a British invasion imminent, Jonathan and Eliza were married by her brother-in-law, Beverly Waugh, at a private wedding in Washington in April of 1814. Jonathan then took Eliza to his home outside Philadelphia to introduce her to his family. In their carriage with four horses, a liveryman, a colored servant for Eliza and a young boy announcing their situation, they attracted a great deal of attention along the way. Even his old girl friends back home were impressed with Eliza.

Next it was young Mary Bushby's turn to be noticed. Edward Fitzgerald, then in his thirties, was a Navy purser who had been assigned to the Washington Naval Yard where he had a chance to meet William Bushby and some of the Carbery clan. He and Thomas Carbery Jr. became lifelong friends[29] and his sister, Anne Marie Fitzgerald, became a close friend of miracle Ann Carbery Mattingly, Thomas's sister.

For some time, Edward had been attracted to the Bushby's youngest daughter, Mary. Now that she was nineteen, he wanted to

---

29 Thomas Carbery was his agent/executor per subsequent ads to sell his property on his death in Georgetown in 1857.

propose to her. He had just gotten back from a tour of duty with the USS *John Adams* when he attended the wedding of Jonathan and Eliza. Not finding an opportunity at the wedding, he wrote her a proposal letter three days later.[lviii] Both Mary and her mother thought highly of Edward and she responded warmly but his duties often carried him elsewhere. With him off to battle Britain in the Great Lakes, he and young Mary continued to correspond and soon had an understanding that they would marry. He asked her to watch over his sister, Anne Marie, while he was away.

In the summer of 1814 when a British invasion of Washington became imminent, Mary Bushby left her boarding house to be run by the staff and took a house near to the Waugh family in Clarksburg, taking her daughter, Mary, with her. Washington was captured by British forces in August. President Madison and his wife spent the night in a town north of Washington called Brookeville in the house shown in figure 23.[30] The British burned parts of the city but then left to pursue the disarranged American army northward toward Baltimore.

Figure 23
Madison Stayed Here in Brookeville in August 1814

---

30   My sister, Anne Fox, is in the foreground.

Many Navy Yard personnel had left to join the army and holding the Navy Yard appeared impossible. Commodore Tingey, seeing the smoke from the burning capitol, ordered the Yard burned to prevent its capture by the enemy. An eyewitness wrote, "No pen can describe the appalling sound that our ears heard and the sight our eyes saw. We could see everything from the upper part of our house as plainly as if we had been in the Yard. All the vessels of war on fire—the immense quantity of dry timber, together with the houses and stores in flames produced an almost meridian brightness. You never saw a drawing room so brilliantly lighted as the whole city was that night." After this, the main shipbuilding function was transferred to the Norfolk, Virginia, Navy Yard, which could handle larger ships, and the Washington Navy Yard concentrated on ordnance and technology.

Congress was to reassemble in September so Jonathan Roberts brought Eliza back down to join her mother in Clarksburg, while he pursued his senatorial duties in Washington. An eventful trip—they heard the bombardment of Fort McHenry as they passed Baltimore. But Baltimore was really a victory for the United States, leading up to the final victory in New Orleans that next January.

By staying in Clarksburg, Eliza was forced to miss a dinner invitation with the president. Jonathan writes that she had already paid her respects to Mrs. Madison. You have to wonder what Dolley Madison and Eliza Roberts talked about. Jonathan Roberts was a close ally of President Madison, often seeing him several times a week, but nowhere in his account does he seem to recognize that his mother-in-law had connections to the Madison family.

A VISIT TO WEST VIRGINIA

I n the fall of 1814, Mary's son, Jacob Hite Manning, wrote to his mother at Clarksburg, asking if he could come there and bring her and Eliza out to Jefferson County to stay with him at Woodlawn, where they would be more comfortable. They agreed. The Waughs were now raising four children of their own in Clarksburg and had no objections.

Now at Woodlawn, in what is now the panhandle of West Virginia, Betsy Roberts (her mother called her that) was expecting a child and wanted to see her husband. In the middle of January, Jonathan made the difficult trip from Washington out to Jefferson County to see her. This was normally an overnight trip, using the Monocacy Ferry and Harper's Ferry, but it took Jonathan three days and he was exhausted when he finally arrived.

He stayed there a week meeting some "interesting guests." They all also had dinner with the Hites. This would be Mary's younger half-brother, George Hite, and his wife, Deborah Rutherford, who lived nearby in Charles Town. Deborah Rutherford Hite and Jacob Hite Manning's wife, Mary Rutherford (nee Darke), had an interesting relationship. Mary was the widow of Thomas Rutherford who appears to have been Deborah Rutherford's first cousin. Just to confuse things further, she went by the name Polly.

There is no mention of their conversation or of George being the president's first cousin. Though Roberts's journal is very precise on political issues concerning President Madison, this connection does not seem to have registered. Jonathan then returned to Washington for the next session of Congress early in February.

A letter he wrote to Eliza on January 21, 2015, just after arriving back in Washington, is quite revealing. After telling of his safe arrival, fatigued but in good spirits, he tells how Cousin Nancy has mended his socks and how much he misses Eliza.

He then writes: "Mr. Engle says he has seen Mrs. Lynch and she says since the burning of the Navy Yard she requires half the rent to be stricken off. He says it has been usual Mr. Carbery gets his so. He wishes Mother's instructions as to what he must do respecting it. He thinks he can raise the 50 dollars by the last of February—Mr. Lovejoy told him to call again but presented him no money. Mr. Engle, however, has seen Mr. Barth and Mr. Bao to give him an answer soon—I must send Ma a stamp to review her Note towards the last of Feb. The stamp she sent is wrong dated—Adieu my love it is time I over away to my seat—A sweet kiss for thyself and the warmest love for our dear cousin ones."

Mary was now moving from home to home and helping her daughters raise grandchildren but she still had boardinghouse business to attend to. Mr. Engle was her rent collector and was finding things a bit difficult. Both Senator Roberts and Reverend Waugh were helping Mary Bushby pay off her financial debts and some of the legal tangles extended into the 1830s.

A THIRD WEDDING

E dward Fitzgerald was planning to marry young Mary Bushby as soon as possible. He talked to Jonathan on his return to Washington and learned that Jacob and Polly Manning were less than enthusiastic about having him as a future brother-in-law. He didn't know whether the cause was his being off on naval assignments, his Catholic religion or just his stubbornness—he knew that he pushed people a bit in order to get his way. Feeling very uncomfortable about going out to Woodlawn to get married, he arranged for his friend Thomas Carbery, then twenty-four years old and not yet mayor, to go out to Charles Town and bring Mary back to Clarksburg. Thomas did this and Edward and Mary were married by Reverend Beverly Waugh on the twentieth of February 1815. Edward knew it was unusual for a Catholic to be married by a Methodist minister but after all, Beverly Waugh was his future brother-in-law and time was of the essence.

In early March, the congressional session having ended, Jonathan Roberts went out to Woodlawn again to greet his new son, Matthew Thomas Roberts, bringing letters from the Fitzgeralds telling of their happiness. Mary immediately wrote back to her daughter and new son-in-law the letter reproduced below, blessing their marriage.

My Dear Children Woodlawn, March 20
It is with heartfelt pleasure that I
acknowledge the receipt of your letters assuring

me that you are mutually pleas'd with each other. Nothing could be more gratifying to the feelings of a fond parent than this knowledge when they have parted with a child in marriage. I gave you up my daughter with a confidence that you want to be happy in each other knowing no other motive than that of affection could influence you and was well assur'd hers was not less disinterested. Your mother's prayer shall be that your happiness may be increas'd in proportion to the rapid increase of your love. On my telling Mr. R. and Betsy that you lov'd so much more than when you married they laugh'd and observ'd they thought it a natural consequence from their own experience. They with Jacob and Polly are much pleas'd to hear of your happiness.

Betsy has a fine son, that she thinks very beautiful, that she would be glad to present you before her return but unless you could meet her at Clarksburg there is little chance as it will be out of her power to go to Washington. Mr. R has left here some days and expected to return in 6 weeks.

I am very desireous of going below first and must leave here as soon as Betsy's situation will justify it. In the meantime if there is any probability of selling the little furniture I have there I should be very much oblig'd to you to dispose of it, as my stay there will be short and there are some debts due that I should not feel long to leave unsettled if I can possibly settle them. The press Mary may offer to Nathins for 30 dollars tho' it is much below its value. If I do not succeed in obtaining some money, I must leave the city with mortification. I shall try to dispose of what I have in Clarksburg before Mr. Waugh leaves there.

Receive my dear children your mother's love accompany'd with her blessings, and a sincere wish that you may never have to combat with the same vicissitudes that she has encounter'd. Your relations unite in love to you both. Your Uncle Hite's family or a part of them were here yesterday. Betsy and Polly send you a kiss each and the former one for her son.

Your truly affectionate mother, Mary Bushby

Give our love to all our friends.

The original letter is shown below in figures 24a and 24b.

My Dear Children   Woodlawn March 20th

it is with heart felt pleasure I ack
nowledge the receipt of your letters assureing me that
you are mutually pleas'd with each other, nothing
could be more gratifying to the feelings of a fond parent
than this knowledge when they have parted with a Child
in Marriage. I gave you up My Daughter with a confi
dence that you would be happy in each other knowing
no other Motive than that of Affection could influence
you and her was well assur'd hers was not less disinter
ested. Your Mothers prayer shall be that your hap-
=piness may be encreas'd in proportion to the rapid
encrease of your love.   on My telling Mr. M and Betty
that you lov'd so much more than when you Married
they laugh'd and observ'd they thought it a natural
consequence from their own experience, they with
Jacob and Polly are much pleas'd to hear of your hap
piness.   Betsy has a fine Son that she thinks
very beautiful, that she would be glad to present
you before her return, but unless you could Meet her at
Clarksburg there is little chance as it will be out of
her power to go to Washington Mr. R has left here
some Days and expects to return in 6 weeks.
I am very desireous of going below first and must

here as soon as Betsy's situation will justify in the meantime if there is any probability of selling the little furniture I have there I should be very much oblig'd to you to dispose of it, as my stay there will be short and there are some debts due that I should not feel easy to leave unsettled if I can possibly discharge them. the press Mary may offer to Mr Watkins for 30 Dollars tho' it is much below its value if I do not succeed in Obtaining some money I must leave the City with Mortification I shall try to dispose of what I have in Clarksburg before Mr Waugh leaves there.

receive My Dear Children your Mothers love accompany'd with her blessing, and a sincere wish that you may never have to Combat with the same Vicissitudes in life that She has encounter'd your Relations unite in love to you Both, your uncle Feites family or a part of them were here yesterday Betsy & Polly Send you a kiss each and the former one for her Son

        Your truly Affectionate Mother
           Mary Bushly

give our love to all our friends

Figure 24b

The letter tells a lot about Mary. She carefully includes the Roberts, the Hites and the Mannings in her felicitations, skirting around the original objections of Jacob and Polly. Social and religious differences do not seem to have been an issue for Mary. Her letter also told her daughter-in-law, Mary Fitzgerald, in Washington, to sell her remaining furniture so that she could pay off her debts, which had mounted, and said that she would return to Washington as soon as Betsy's condition permitted but would not stay long.

Jonathan had already left to check on things back home in Pennsylvania but promised to come back in six weeks and bring all of them home with him to Norristown. Before he could do that, however, Mary Manning Bushby returned to Washington to clear up her affairs. By this time, Eliza and the new baby were ready to travel with her and she left them at the Waughs in Maryland. In late May, Jonathan hired a horse and carriage in Pennsylvania and went to pick up his wife and baby, along with Cousin Nancy Bushby, at Clarksburg and took them down to Washington. There they, in turn, picked up Mary and headed back to Norristown. This was a six-day trip; Jonathan taking the three ladies and a baby and going home by way of Baltimore, York, the Susquehanna River bridge and Lancaster.

NEW GRANDCHILDREN KEEP COMING

Mary was now sixty-one years old and ready to slow down but grandbabies kept coming along for her to care for. Her daughter, Eliza, had soon given birth to a second child, a daughter named Mary Catherine Roberts. Mary Fitzgerald was also pregnant and had come up to Norristown to be with her mother and Eliza. Edward was in New York, getting the USS *Java* ready for a Mediterranean assignment, when young Edward Harris Fitzgerald arrived on the scene on December 23, 1815. The naval purser exchanged some excited letters with Ma and Eliza but could not be present, even though it was then the Christmas holidays.

1816 went along smoothly enough. They did get to see Edward before he left but he was soon cruising the Mediterranean Sea with Captain Oliver Hazard Perry. He wrote a long letter to Jonathan in July telling of Perry's tactful dealings with the Dey of Algiers, who quite incorrectly felt that a treaty had been violated. Edward's wife, Mary, was still in Norristown at that time but had decided to move back to Washington where Edward's sister and mother were living together. She set up housekeeping on New Jersey Avenue in the Capitol Hill area of Washington.

This was still not the end of Mary Hite Manning Bushby's travels and 1817 was a troubled year. Her son, Jacob, and her half-brother, George Hite, had both died late in 1816 and Edward Fitzgerald's mother died early in 1817. In March 1817, Edward wrote from

Newport, Rhode Island, urging Mary, in Washington, to get Anne Maria Fitzgerald to sell her place and move in with Mary. The place began to fill up. Mary Bushby, now age sixty-three, came down to visit when her daughter's second child, Mary Ann Jane Fitzgerald, was born. There was still plenty of work for Ma to do.

Both of the Roberts children died of the cholera in August of 1817. Eliza, devastated, went to visit her mother who was still in Washington with the Fitzgeralds. When she returned home to Pennsylvania, she brought Mary Bushby back with her. Mary Hite Manning Bushby was certainly beginning to feel her age but was really doing quite well until the following January when right after the birth of Eliza's second son, William Roberts, Mary fell into a deep paralysis from which she never recovered. Jonathan came home in time to witness her death on February 3, 1818.

Her obituary in a Washington, DC, newspaper read as follows: "The deceased bore her painful illness of some weeks' continuance with that sweetness of temper and that pious fortitude of mind which had distinguished her and endeared her to numerous friends through a life checquered with the sorest trials which are inflicted by the chastening hand of a just and merciful Providence."

AFTER MARY'S DEATH

Mary Hite's story does not really end with her death. Things set in motion by her second marriage and her move to Washington continued to evolve over time. The culmination of all this occurred when her namesake granddaughter, Mary Hite Manning, married into the Carbery family.

Euphemia Lacy Manning, Mary's daughter-in-law, had somehow gotten into the Bushby/Carbery circle of friends. The record is not clear exactly how this occurred but after all, Mary Bushby Fitzgerald and Euphemia's husband, Nathaniel, were half-siblings. Edward Fitzgerald's best friend was Thomas Carbery. Edward's sister was a close friend of Ann Carbery Mattingly and was present in her bedroom when the miraculous recovery from cancer occurred on March 10, 1824. Both Edward's wife, Mary, and his sister, Anne Maria, gave affidavits telling of their knowledge of the miracle and saying they had known Mrs. Mattingly closely for ten and fourteen years, respectively. All this was clear to Euphemia.

The Visitation Convent in Georgetown and the Visitation Academy for Young Women appears to have played an important role. Ann Carbery Mattingly was a frequent visitor to this convent and it seems inevitable that her daughter, Mary Susan, attended the Visitation Academy. Mary Hite Manning's obituary strongly suggests that she was a student at the Visitation Academy[31] and she and Mary

---

31   Mary H. Manning's obituary states that, "she had been trained in a school where the painful but necessary maxims of self-denial are inculcated, and

Susan Mattingly were roughly the same age.[32] There was obviously a connection made because in 1826, Mary Hite Manning became a Catholic and married Mary Susan Mattingly's uncle Thomas Carbery, ex-mayor of Washington.[33] He was age thirty-five and she was age twenty-two.

Quite possibly, Euphemia Manning heard about the Visitation Academy from the Fitzgeralds and convinced her husband, Nathaniel, to send their daughters there. It was quite common for non-Catholic families to send their daughters to this excellent school, often with unexpected conversions occurring as a result.[lix] Founded in 1799 by Archbishop Leonard Neale (figure 14), president of Georgetown College, and three Visitation nuns from Visitation Convent, this is now the Georgetown Visitation Preparatory School. Figure 20 shows how the rebuilt Visitation Convent and Academy looked in 1895, some seventy years after Mary Susan Mattingly and Mary Hite Manning would have attended.

Another relative who converted was Margaret Hite, born in 1793, daughter of Mary Manning Bushby's half-brother, George Hite. According to a 1920 magazine article:

> "Margaret accompanied her brother, Robert, to Washington in 1825, where she made the acquaintance of a devout Catholic family (whose name has not come down to us), through

therefore she had resigned to bend her will to that of her heavenly father."

32   An attempt was made to verify this by contacting the school but owing to a devastating fire at the convent in 1993, much of the early archives have been lost. The only recognizable names found were Helen Carbery (1836) and Martha Carbery (1837), daughters of James and Lewis Carbery. We know from other sources that Edward and Mary Bushby Fitzgerald's daughter attended Visitation.

33   Unfortunately, the Manning/Carbery marriage was beset with health problems. They had four children before she died in 1834 but none of the children lived more than ten years. We saw the same problem with the first few children of Eliza and Jonathan Roberts. Sanitary conditions were none too good in those days.

whose exemplary life she at length became attracted to their religion. After much prayer and study she at last was given the great grace of conversion. Following her baptism in 1827, she entered the Visitation Convent at Georgetown. She pronounced her vows on the Feast of S. Jane Frances de Chantal, August 21, 1828, receiving the name of Sister Mary Theonella."[lx]

That devout Catholic family may have been a mystery to the writer but it is pretty clear that Ann Carbery Mattingly's miracle, in 1824, had something to do with Margaret Hite's conversion.

Obviously, the West Virginia Mannings were in close contact with their DC cousins. When Mary's grandson, Nathaniel William Manning (figure 19), married Martha Price Craighill in 1835, the marriage was performed in Georgetown,[lxi] fifty miles away from home, to accommodate the many cousins living in Washington.

In Warner's book on Catholics in the new capital city, he gives many examples of mixed marriages and, often, the Carberys were involved.[lxii] When Edward Fitzgerald married Mary Bushby, she was not a Catholic but the evidence is quite clear that she eventually became one. Their daughter Mary Ann Jane Fitzgerald attended the Visitation Academy in Georgetown. She married John Doyle, a Catholic, and several of the Doyle children went to Catholic boarding schools in Frederick and Baltimore, Maryland. Another daughter, Emily Catherine Fitzgerald, entered the convent as a nun.

The Washington Navy Yard was not really well suited to ship building and was converted to ordinance manufacture in the 1820s so Edward and Mary Fitzgerald moved on to Norfolk, Virginia, where they raised their family. After his wife and several children died in the smallpox epidemic of 1855, Edward moved back to Georgetown where he died in 1857 at the age of 75. He maintained his friendship with Thomas Carbery to the end and Carbery was named executor of his will.

The religious preferences that show up in Mary's story are fascinating. A great deal of comment has been made over the history of religious intolerance in the thirteen colonies and religious unrest continued well into the nineteenth century.[lxiii] You would not know it from this story. The Mannings were Baptists originally, but Reverend Nathaniel Manning attended a Presbyterian college and became an Anglican minister. Mary's Hite ancestry was German Lutheran and probably Irish Presbyterian but Mary's two husbands set the religious commitment for her family. Some of her Hite cousins became Methodists. William Bushby, a devout Methodist, must have known about the Georgetown Catholic Church's acquisition of the Methodist meeting place in Alexandria and probably was personally involved. Three Bushby daughters married a Methodist minister, a non-practicing Quaker and a Catholic, and the latter two marriages were performed by the Methodist minister. A Catholic being married by a future Methodist bishop is quite a novelty but there is no question that the Fitzgeralds were Catholics. Edward was certainly one of those Catholics who accommodated his non-Catholic friends and relatives. He was a Mason and a founding member of their Navy Lodge.

Mary's son, Nathaniel Manning, was married in Leesburg, Virginia, by a Methodist Episcopal minister named John Littlejohn and Nathaniel later became a Presbyterian church trustee. Euphemia's parents were Quakers. Yet three of Nathaniel and Euphemia Manning's daughters married Washington, DC, Catholics. Mary Hite Manning married ex-Mayor Thomas Carbery in 1826, Catherine A. Manning married Edward Neale Roach in 1839 and Margaret Hite Manning married William Edward Greenwell in 1854. All three men were from old St. Mary's County Catholic families. A relative of Bishop Neale (figure 14), Roach was Commissioner of Wills and Administrator of the Orphans Court in Washington. Figure 25 is a photo of their daughter, Annie Euphemia Roach, Mary Hite's great granddaughter who married Coast Guard Captain Thomas Wolcott Lay. Greenwell was also a Coast Guard Captain.[lxiv] He moved with his wife, Margaret, to San Francisco where she died in childbirth. He then married a woman who was a known Visitation Academy graduate. Three other Manning girls married men named Colt, Reardon, and Cochran, the last two quite possibly Catholic names. Ellen Cochran ended up raising Greenwell and Colt children after their mothers had died and, in turn, was rewarded in her own mother's will.

Figure 25
Annie Euphemia Roach Lay

The story of Ann Carbery Mattingly's son, John, a Georgetown College student who eloped with a mixed-race woman in 1826 and was ostracized from his family, was told in *Growing with America: Colonial Roots*. They eloped out to Moorefield, where Mary Hite Manning Bushby had started family life. Their son, Thomas Joseph Mattingly, was born there on June 2, 1827.[lxv] But how did John Mattingly meet Harriet Doyle and how did they hear about Moorefield, which today has a population of under 2,600 people? Could it have been one of the slaves that Mary and William Bushby released in 1788 and 1789? It seems probable that some of them stayed on as personal servants, freemen, not slaves. We do know that the family kept track of these former slaves, with Mary Fitzgerald intervening to stop the return to slavery of one of their daughters in 1824.[lxvi]

Euphemia Manning is a story in herself. When her eldest daughter Mary became a Catholic to marry Mayor Thomas Carbery, Euphemia became a Catholic too. She was baptized a Catholic at St. Patrick's Church in Washington, DC, on October 15, 1827.[34] After

---

34   Baptismal records of St. Patrick's Church, Washington.

her husband died in 1830, she moved to Washington to be near her daughters. Sometime before 1850, Euphemia Manning bought the three-story brick house on Thirteenth Street in Washington's Ward 2 that she bequeathed in her will to her unmarried daughter, Sallie. One 1850 census has her living in Loudoun County with her twenty-one-year-old son Jacob but another has her living in Washington's Second Ward with her daughter Sallie and a host of other characters. Some of these people may have been servants but Euphemia had excellent connections now in the city and she and her daughter appear to have been running a boardinghouse. Perhaps she had gotten that idea from her mother-in-law.

She had inherited that 600-plus acre farm in Loudoun County that her father had left Nathaniel and income from the farm was enough to sustain a satisfactory way of living. She left the farm to her children and in 1883, her son Jacob, her executor, and his sister, Ellen Cochran, sold it to developers. It became Paeonian Springs, a housing project aimed at rich folk from the capital city. The Washington and Old Dominion Railroad line had come through there in 1860 and it was an easy commute. The development died out in the early 1900s but in 2006, Paeonian Springs was named a National Historic District. Figure 26 is a photo of the memorial marker at the former train station.

And what about Mary's grandson, Jacob? He became the hard-luck post–Civil War farmer in a recent (2,000) book on farming trends in Virginia.[lxvii] There is much more to tell about Mary Hite's descendants but we'll have to leave it there for now. You can find all that in my book, *Growing with America: Colonial Roots.*

The Washington & Old Dominion Railroad Regional Park • Northern Virginia Regional Park Authority

Paeonian Springs Station

In its heyday, Paeonian Springs attracted folks such as these men gathered for a raccoon hunt sponsored by *The Washington Post* in October 1912. The station shown at right stood where the three-sided shelter stands today.

Two things happened to make places like Paeonian Springs popular. The first was the need to escape heat and epidemics such as the ones that hit Washington in the 1860s and 70s. The second was the expansion of the railroads, making travel easy and inexpensive. The railroad arrived here in 1871.

Paeonian Springs promoted its "healing" springs, which people drank from and bathed in. For ten cents you could buy a gallon to take with you—and bottles were shipped to Washington by rail. By 1912 a boardwalk linked the depot with "downtown," which consisted of a post office, a confectionery store, a mill, a blacksmith shop, a wheelwright shop, a general store, and three boarding houses.

Above: The original station.
Below: Raccoon hunters gather beside the station in October 1912.

Figure 26
Memorial Marker at Location of the Former
Paeonian Springs Train Station

ILLUSTRATIONS

THE PHOTOS ON THE COVER

There are no known portraits of Mary Hite but we do have several of her relatives and descendants. Look at cousin Isaac Hite Jr. in figure 8, see grandson Nathaniel Manning in figure 19 and son Jacob Hite Manning on the cover of *Growing with America*. To add to this, there is a photo of Annie Euphemia Roach, Mary Hite's great-granddaughter shown in figure 25. There are certain facial features common to all of these people and on this basis, I have picked a photo of my sister, Mardy Rawls, to represent young Mary Hite on the front cover and a watercolor portrait that Mardy did of our grandmother, Annie Carbery Lay, to represent old Mary Hite on the back cover of this book.

TIMELINES

Mary Hite's story covers a lot of ground and the number of factual traces left behind is really quite amazing. Bare facts, however, don't always tell the full story. In telling Mary's story, some liberties have been taken in the interpretation of these facts and perhaps it is time for a brief recapitulation. A timeline containing the known facts often can be quite revealing. Here we present one for Mary Hite Manning Bushby and one for Jonathan Roberts and Edward Fitzgerald taken from Robert's memoirs and Fitzgerald's letters over the years of interest.

While the location of Reverend Mannings' Glebe and Fort Pleasant are well defined by the 1854 Poor Farm document and the hand-drawn map, the Mannings' life out there is largely based on inference from known facts about the area and the doings of the Abraham Hite family. The same goes for Mary's trip back out there with her sons in 1784—she would certainly have had to take them but there is no direct proof. The birth of Nathaniel Manning, Jr., in Shenandoah County is well documented but it is not known who came with her, where Mary actually stayed and how long. The same is true of where Mary actually stayed and taught children when she went back to Berkeley County. There are hints but no actual facts aside from her signing her brother's will and the Orphan Papers showing her payments for schooling. And of course, how she met William Bushby is fictional.

As for her childhood, the facts are minimal but the interpretation is pretty straightforward, except for the large gathering of family and friends after the death of Jost Hite. Here I will admit to being influenced by Minnie Hite Moody's semi-fictional book, *Long Meadows*. She describes a very large gathering with a great deal of discussion as to where Jost should be buried, ending up with a decision to bury him in the graveyard of the Lutheran Church in Winchester.[lxviii] This is pure fiction, of course. We don't really know where he is buried. The large gathering does seem reasonable, however, and I've taken the idea and run with it.

The concern of the Hite family over James Madison's efforts on behalf of the United States Constitution in 1787 is another matter of conjecture. It is known, however, that Alexander White, stepfather of Mary's nieces, was one of the doubters. He was a Virginia Representative to Congress from 1789 to 1793 and later a member of the commission to plan the construction of Washington, DC. He wrote some twenty-two letters to James Madison over the period from 1788 to 1795, all supportive of Madison's efforts but admitting to have been a doubter in 1787 when Madison was writing the United States Constitution.

The latter part of Mary Manning's story, while relying heavily on Jonathan Robert's Journal and Fitzgerald's letters, also makes a few assumptions when it comes to personal relationships. It seems obvious that Edward Fitzgerald would have attended Jonathan's wedding though definitive evidence is lacking. He did write his letter to his future wife, Mary Bushby, shortly thereafter. The friendship between the Catholic Fitzgeralds and the Catholic Carberys is well established. How close the Bushbys and the Carberys were before Edward married Mary is matter of speculation. The men did work together at the Navy Yard and live together in Georgetown for a while. After Edward Fitzgerald married the Bushby daughter, Mary, in 1814, the connection became closer.

Mary Hite Manning Bushby Timeline

About 1754: Born in Frederick County, Virginia, to Jacob Hite and Catherine O'Bannon. Date based on information in her 1818 obituary.

1760 Age 6: Her mother dies.

1761 Age 7: Her grandfather, Jost Hite, dies.

December 15, 1761: Her father remarries, this time to Frances Madison Beale (aunt of James Madison who became President Madison in 1809) in Orange County, Virginia.

December 22, 1763: Mary's sister Elizabeth, age twenty, is married to her stepbrother, Tavener Beale Jr., age 21.

Late 1760s: Jacob Hite and his partner Richard Pearis scheme to obtain 150,000 acres of land from the Cherokee Indians in South Carolina. A British official gets South Carolina to void the deal, leaving Hite in debt.

March 7, 1770: Jacob Hite makes out his will. In it, he leaves to his daughter Mary, then sixteen, "the lands and plantations on Opequon bought of Joseph Beeler* whereon now live Benjamin Wittell, Benjamin Wallingsford, Widow Craven, Thomas Ball, John Gooding and Widow Leister" or 1,000 pounds current money of Virginia at her discretion. This was probably the 751 acres Beeler had obtained in a 1769 land grant. He then divides his estate among his sons and daughters by name. This will was apparently not proven until 1779 when Thomas Hite found it.

December 22, 1771: In a codicil to the above will, Jacob leaves his one-sixth share of the brigantine *Swift* and her cargo and one-eight share of the schooner *Friendship*. He also provides for the care and schooling of underage children. Executors are his wife Frances, his sons Thomas and John and James Keith as executors. Witnesses include Abraham Hite and his daughter Sarah. This will was not found until 1779. Meanwhile, his son John Hite assumes he inherits the South Carolina properties.

March 16, 1772: Nathaniel Manning, William Leigh and Robert Buchan are ordained ministers of the Anglican Church in London.

Mar 27, 1772: Nathaniel Manning receives twenty pounds to pay for his return voyage from England where he had been ordained. He had been practicing medicine in New Jersey from 1762 until 1771.

May 19, 1772: Jacob Hite named one of the Justices of Newly formed Berkeley County, Virginia.

1772, Age 17: Mary's marriage to Rev. Nathaniel Manning was probably in the summer of 1772. They move to The Glebe, where Nathaniel becomes pastor of Hampshire Parish. The Glebe is known to have been Lot 5 in Lord Fairfax's South Branch Manor located on the "Indian Old Fields" just north of Moorefield and not far from her uncle Abraham Hite's residence at Fort Pleasant. The Glebe eventually became the Hardy County Poor Farm. This was near the head of The Trough, a seven-mile stretch of the South Branch of the Potomac River where it cuts through the Allegheny Mountains flowing north.

October 15, 1772: Berkeley County Sheriff Adam Stephens put up for sale by Public Venue Jacob Hite's 3,118-acre plantation in Berkeley County in order to pay his debts. Hite threatens to sue. Around this same time, Jacob deeds 842 acres to his daughter Mary and her husband Reverend Nathaniel Manning.

November 10, 1772: Mary's brother Thomas, age twenty-two, is married to his stepsister, Frances Madison Beale, age twenty-three.

1773: Angered at having Martinsburg, rather than Leesburg, named capital of Berkeley County, Jacob Hite established his residence in South Carolina.

January 12, 1774: Hampshire County will of Reverend Nathaniel Manning gives to Mary (and her heirs) property on Opecken Creek that was given to him in 1772 by Jacob Hite as well as all remainder of his estate. Mary is executrix and Abraham Hite and Thomas Hite are co-executors. No mention of a life estate. Witnesses are Abraham Hite, Abraham Hite Jr., and J. Hite 2nd.

April 14, 1774: Jacob Hite's friends along with his son, Thomas, raid the Martinsburg Jail freeing horses and slaves. Jacob then sends his 210 slaves off to his property in South Carolina. Legal and verbal battles with Stephens go on through 1775 when Stephens heads off to fight in the Revolutionary War.

June 21, 1774 Age 20: Mary's first son, Jacob Hite Manning, is born in Hampshire County, West Virginia. He was married in Berkshire County in 1798 and eventually lived in Charles Town, Jefferson County.

1775: Jacob and Frances Hite are selling property in Alexandria, Virginia, located near the boat harbor and proximate to where a painter named William Bushby owns property.

Jan 12, 1776 Age 22: Mary's second son, Nathaniel Manning, is born and baptized in Shenandoah County, Virginia. This county is located south of Winchester, Virginia, some fifty to sixty miles from Moorefield on today's roads. Mary had Bowman cousins living in Shenandoah County. Perhaps she went there for help during childbirth.

July 1, 1776: Mary's father, Jacob Hite, his wife and most of his family die in Greenville County, South Carolina, at the hands of Cherokee Indians.

October 25, 1776: Mary is given a riding chair and horse the value of fifty pounds and a mourning ring in the will of her brother, John Hite. He divides the South Carolina property among his brothers and sisters.

February 1777 Age 23: Mary's husband, Reverend Nathaniel Manning, dies in Hampshire County, Virginia. Her husband and father are now dead and she is left with two children, one and two years old. Best evidence is that she moves back to Berkeley County.

February 11, 1777: Bond to Hampshire Court for 2,000 pounds, signed by Abel Randall and Mary Manning. Mary is executrix of the will of Nathaniel Manning.

March 18, 1777: John Hite's will is executed in Berkeley County Court.

September 22, 1778: Mary Manning is witness to the will of her brother, Thomas Hite, in Berkeley County. Berkeley County Will Book 1 p 172. Executors were his wife, Francis Madison Beale Hite, her sister, Elizabeth Beale Harrison and her husband, George Harrison, of Madison County, Virginia.

1778: Guessing that she had to move from the Glebe; she received in Reverend Manning's will the 200 acres in Berkeley County on Opeken (Opequon) Creek that the Reverend Nathaniel received of Jacob Hite, her father.

August 17, 1779: Mary Manning is a witness in Berkeley court attesting to the will of her brother, Thomas Hite, deceased.

1784 Age 30: Mary Manning, widow of Berkeley Co, bought Lot No 17 from the Trustees of the Town of Moorefield that she might erect thereon a residence. She bought from a "quantity of land to be laid off in lots of 1/2 acre" Isaac Hite also bought. While there was a two-year period for building a house, this was relaxed and there is no evidence that Mary ever built one though she paid taxes through 1789. Moorefield was founded in 1777 and is where another fork enters the south fork of the Potomac. It is in Hardy County, West Virginia, west and south of Berkeley and Jefferson Counties in the panhandle of West Virginia. Her property is now the site of the Hardy County Courthouse.

May 1785: Trinity Methodist church leaders arranged a personal interview with General George Washington at Mount Vernon for the Bishops Thomas Coke and Francis Asbury, who met at William Bushby's house in Alexandria before traveling on to meet with the general regarding the emancipation of slaves.[35] William Bushby had several slaves, mostly with children and, by 1790, had granted them conditional freedom based on them reaching a certain age.

September 1785 to April 1787: Mrs. Manning is providing schooling and board for the three orphan daughters of her brother John Hite; Catherine, Mary and Susan Hite arranged for by their guardians Alexander White and his wife, Sarah Nichols Hite. Alexander was a lawyer in Winchester. There seems little doubt that this was Mary Manning and she was probably living near her old home in Berkeley County.

---

35   Stukenbroeker, Fern C. 1974. A Watermelon for God. Alexandria, Virginia. p 22.

February 20, 1785: Mrs. Manning is paid for sundries purchased in Shepherdstown just to the north of New Hopewell. Jefferson County did not exist in 1777 but Shepherdstown was the oldest town in the area.

February 5, 1788 Age 34: She is married again, this time to William Bushby. Mary is thirty-four and William is forty-two.

February 17, 1789[36]: William Bushby manumits and discharges from future service a Negro woman named Sarah, thirty-five years of age.

March 10, 1790 Age 36: Daughter Eliza Hite Bushby is born.

September 20, 1790: William Bushby "presents absolutely manumit and discharge from Bondage and further service as slaves upon the following terms and conditions the hereafter named Negroes, to wit; Mary, now of the age of twenty five years to go free immediately, Milly being now twenty seven years old to be free in five years [1795], Cloe now twenty one years old to be free in seven years [1797], David now thirteen years old to be free in twelve years [1802], Ned now being twelve years old to be free in thirteen years [1803], Nancy being now eight years old to be free in seventeen years [1807], Rachel being now eight years old to be free in seventeen years [1807], George being now five years old to be free in twenty years [1810], Betty being now two years old to be free in twenty three years [1813], and Molly being now one year old to be free in twenty four years [1814].[37]"

September 4, 1791 Age 37: Daughter Catherine Bruce Bushby is born.

February 14, 1795: Age 38: Daughter Mary Hite Bushby is born.

September 25, 1798: Her oldest son, Jacob Hite Manning, marries Mary Darke of Berkeley County, West Virginia. They live in Charles Town, Jefferson, West Virginia (then Virginia).

1799: Intending to move to Georgetown to enhance his painting and glazing business, Bushby sells property five miles from river, probably in Alexandria, Virginia. He also offers for rent

36   Fairfax County Deed Book R, pages 342–343.
37   Fairfax County Deed Book S, pages 532–533.

his four-room brick house seven miles from river on an acre of land with a one-acre garden fenced in. Apparently, this is on 170 acres which is offered for lease.

1800: Residence Georgetown, Washington, DC.

1801 Age 47: Some say a son William Bushby is born, nothing more known about him except that a William Bushby appears in legal documents in the 1830s.

April 26, 1803 Age 49: Her son Nathaniel Manning Jr. marries Euphemia Lacy and they are living in Loudoun County until he dies in 1830 (Middleburg in 1820, Hillsboro in 1830). They are married by Reverend Littlejohn of the Methodist Episcopal Church. In the 1850 census, Euphemia is registered in Loudoun County (Paeonian Springs, near Leesburg) living with her son, Jacob Hite Manning, who is twenty-one and in Washington, DC, living with a bunch of possible renters. Jacob marries in 1855.

September 24, 1805: William Bushby writes letter to James Madison, then Secretary of State, referring to a previous letter of recommendation from George Hite, Mary's half-brother, requesting aid in re-employment at the Navy Yard. States that he has purchased property near the Naval Yard, presumably that property on M Street between Tenth and Eleventh referred to in his will.

June 6, 1810: Will of William Bushby states: "I therefore give and desire to my faithful wife, Mary Bushby and ordain her the sole executrix of this my last will and testament, all my real and personal property, whether of Lands, Moneys, Goods, etc. to her and to her heirs and assigns for ever to be applied by her agreeable to her own judgment."

July 1810: Mary's husband William Bushby dies. Mary is fifty-six and her children are twenty, eighteen, fifteen and (possibly) nine.

1811–1815: Children are born to Jacob Manning and Mary Darke.

1804–1828: Children are born to Nathaniel Manning and Euphemia Lacy. The oldest, Mary H., born in 1804, married Thomas Carbery in 1826. Obituary says she attended a school where self-denial was important and she learned to surrender her will to her Heavenly Father. Sounds like Visitation Academy.

1812 Age 58: Mary's daughter Catherine marries Beverly Waugh, Methodist minister. Mary is living on Capitol Hill in DC running a boarding house with her daughters Eliza and Mary.

April 21, 1814 Age 60: Her daughter Eliza marries Jonathan Roberts. Roberts is a Congressman (Senator to be) from Norristown, Pennsylvania, who was boarding with them.

February 20, 1815 Age 61: Her daughter Mary marries Edward Fitzgerald, brother of Anne Maria Fitzgerald who was present at Ann Carbery Mattingly's miracle (both Mary and Anne Maria gave affidavits pertaining to the truth of the miracle.) The Fitzgeralds were married by her brother-in-law, Reverend Beverly Waugh, at his home in Clarksburg, Maryland.

February 3, 1818 Age 64: Mary dies at the home of Jonathan Roberts in Montgomery Co., Pennsylvania.

1860: Euphemia Manning dies in 1860 in Washington County, Washington, DC, age seventy-four.

Jonathan Roberts–Edward Fitzgerald Timeline

From Roberts' memoirs written to his daughter Sarah Tyson plus Fitzgerald family letters

1813
May 19 to August 9: New Congress Meets
– Gallatin and tax to pay for war are discussed.
Summer
– Lodging with Mary Bushby
– Finds Elizabeth very attractive
– She had a good reputation
– Mary Bushby, Eliza and Mary (later Fitzgerald) made up the family
– Eliza ran things, presided at table
– Eleven or twelve boarders including VA Senator Richard Brent, a drinker
– Wm Sanford, Eliza's suitor, had died during that session of Congress.
August 9 – He goes home

– Eliza has given him a letter to take to her sister Catherine Waugh, in Baltimore. She is not there so he writes Eliza a letter, which she acknowledges and he responds carefully but warmly. Says nothing to Mathew and Mary (Roberts).

Sometime in Fall – He returns, hesitates to go pick up his trunk, she hears he is back and wonders so he goes and meets her, with reserve. They were paying high rent in a house not formed for boarders, boarding cost raised, two boarders contemplate leaving. He is afraid to take room with stove without chimney and worries about compromising her so he tells her he is not boarding with them. They converse and he tells her he wants to marry her and is to become a senator and has a good home for her. She is receptive and so is her mother.

1814: In Washington, people are curious. Congressmen call on her and like her. General Brown gives his benediction and Col. R. M. Johnson, a congressman, applies to Mrs. Bushby for boarding. Roberts is already back there, his other arrangement having fallen through. Eliza likes him, agrees to marry him and changes her view of congressmen, which was pretty bad.

Roberts had intended to return home before he is married but Johnson convinces him not to wait and Eliza (and her mother) agree.

February 28, 1814: He takes his seat in the Senate. War is at its height.

April 21, 1814: Thursday after Congress adjourns they are privately married in Washington, DC, by Reverend Beverly Waugh, her brother-in-law. He has no best man but she has friends of both sexes present. They set out the next morning for Pennsylvania in a carriage with four horses. She has colored servant; he has a boy. They attract much notice on the way. They get there without incident and are welcomed by family and neighbors. Even old girl friends.

Dated April 25 1814, this letter is Edward's marriage proposal to Mary Bushby. His assignment on the USS *John Adams* is over and he now has some money. He has seen her recently, perhaps at her sister's wedding three days before.

Dated May 31, 1814, having left Washington for naval duty as a ship's purser, Edward writes a love letter to Mary from Sacket's Harbor, New York. Introduces his sister (Anne Maria[38] to Mary and sends love to Ma.

August 1814: Washington is captured by the British and burned but the British then leave; Congress to reassemble in September. Mrs. Bushby has given up running the house, disposed of some furniture and taken a house next door to Reverend Beverly Waugh in Clarksburg on the road to Frederick about thirty miles from DC. The Roberts set out for Washington via stage from Paoli. Eventful trip. Columbia: driver drunk, stage gets caught in river. Wrightsville, they learn that the British were just starting to attack Baltimore. York, people retired, Tuesday morning and stage to Frederick not til Saturday; on toward Baltimore; stay in Loveton, bedbugs.

September 13, 1814: British bombardment of Fort McHenry; back to York on Thursday; stage full on Saturday but on to Taneytown overnight then to Frederick. Next day caught great western stage and in ten miles were in Clarksburg. Eliza united with her mother. Roberts on to Washington the next day.

Washington a scene of ruin and desolation but war went well at Baltimore. Opposition tries to embarrass and remove Madison. Eliza comes down to Washington, remains a short time and returns to Clarksburg missing dinner with the president but had met Dolley Madison. Roberts sees Madison two or three times a week. Several visits to Clarksburg to see ladies.

November: Uncle Jacob Manning carried ladies to Woodlawn, some seventy miles further away. This was to make them more comfortable.

1815

January 8, 1815: Battle of New Orleans, war ends.

January 10: Roberts sets out for Woodlawn on horseback in winter. Difficult trip. Monocacy ferry, dinner with Capt. Dixon. Crosses

---

38   Anne Maria Fitzgerald is present when Ann Carbery Mattingly's miracle occurs in 1824 and has known Mrs. Mattingly intimately since about 1810, according to her published affidavit.

Cacoctin Mountain and lodged at Trap town; crosses Harper's Ferry in a bateaux and now seven miles from Manning's. Procures horse and reaches Woodlawn before nightfall. Good welcome, stays a week and is entertained at dinner by George Hite in Charles Town seven miles away.

Leaves via horseback; uneventful trip via Harper's ferry and Monocacy ferry, is very cold but gets back okay. News of peace arrives, much conflict between parties about settlement but finds Madison calm and firm. Does not credit Jackson much for New Orleans. Likes Sen. Macon from NC but dislikes John Randolph.

January 21, 1815: Roberts writes letter to Eliza telling of arrival back in Washington and giving information to Mary about her boardinghouse.

Dated February 2, 1815: Edward, in Washington, writes to Mary, with her mother and sister Betsy (Eliza) Roberts[39] at Jacob Manning's place called Woodlawn, concerning their upcoming wedding. He does not want to come to Woodlawn in Jefferson County, Virginia[40], since her half-brother has objected to the marriage. He prefers Clarksburg, Maryland, where Reverend Waugh (her sister's husband) lives and offers Mr. Carbery's services to escort her there.

February 20, 1815: Mary Bushby and Edward Fitzgerald are married by Reverend Waugh in Clarksburg, Thomas Carbery attending (as best man?)

March 3: Session ends. Jonathan returns to Woodlawn, greeted by Mannings and by birth of son, Mathew Thomas Roberts. Stays only a fortnight, then returns to his home in Pennsylvania via Chambersburg and Carlisle and Harrisburg. Awaits Eliza's coming.

Dated March 20, 1815, Mary Hite Manning Bushby at Woodlawn, writes to Edward and Mary, giving her blessing on their wedding. Says Jacob and Polly approve, and the Roberts do so

---

39   Eliza had married Senator Jonathan Roberts in Washington on April 21, 1814. Reverend Waugh presided.
40   Later West Virginia.

with enthusiasm. Intends to come to Washington temporarily as soon as Betsy's condition permits (the Roberts have a new son) and asks Mary Fitzgerald to dispose of her furniture in Washington as she has debts to repay.

End of May: Jonathan gets horse and carriage and goes to pick up Eliza and baby at Waughs in Clarksburg, a three-day trip. Then went down to Washington to pick up Mary Bushby. Had picked up cousin Nancy at Clarksburg. Remained over Sabbath and then back to Penna. with three ladies and baby leaving them in Norristown. Travels via Baltimore, York, Susquehanna bridge and Lancaster, six days.

June: The Roberts are now in their own house.

Autumn: Back to Washington leaving Eliza with Mary Bushby and Mary Fitzgerald in Norristown (as Edward was off on sea duty and they had yet to find a home.) Daily letters back and forth. Session of Congress: Question of a bank. Much controversy. Insult to Washington by young Randolph. Talked with Biddle. Compensation bill.

Dated December 13, 1815, Edward, in New York, writes to Mary Fitzgerald at the Roberts' home near Norristown concerned about her upcoming delivery.

Dated December 30, 1815, Edward, in New York, writes to Mary thanking her for giving him a son. He is off to the Mediterranean on the USS *Java*.

1816

Dated July 7, 1816, Edward writes to Jonathan Roberts from Gibraltar giving details on his travels with Captain Perry on the USS Java and thanking him for housing Mary.

1817

Dated March 21, 1817, Edward writes from Newport, Rhode Island, to Mary on New Jersey Avenue in Washington[41] (on Capitol Hill) concerning deaths in family, plus housing details and asking her to care for his sister.[42]

---

41 The Thomas Carbery house at Seventeenth and C Streets is a mile away over near the White House.

42 Anne Maria Fitzgerald, a staunch Catholic, continues to live with them

August 1817: Roberts' son Mathew and daughter Mary Catherine die of the cholera. Now childless. Cousin Nancy, Sister Mary and brother Mathew lent every kindness. Eliza wanted to visit her mother who was now in Washington with the Fitzgeralds. When she returned, she brought her mother with her. Jonathan goes back to the Senate in Washington.

1818

January: Son William is born. A week later, Mary Hite Manning Bushby is in severe paralysis.

February 3, 1818" Jonathan returns home and Mary Bushby dies the next day. "On Tuesday the third in the sixty-fourth year of her age at the home of her son-in-law Jonathan Roberts of Montgomery County, Mary Bushby, relict of Mr. William Bushby, late of the city of Washington. The deceased bore her painful illness of some weeks' continuance with that sweetness of temper and that pious fortitude of mind which had distinguished her and endeared her to numerous friends through a life checquered with the sorest trials which are inflicted by the chastening hand of a just and merciful Providence." Obituary in the National Intelligencer.

1821

March 3, 1821: Retires from Senate and returns home. Two or three days later, daughter Mary Anna Roberts dies of the croup, just weaned. Son Mathew has also died.

---

indefinitely. The Fitzgeralds send their daughters to Catholic schools; one of them becomes a nun. On the other hand, they were married by her brother-in-law, Reverend Waugh, a Methodist minister, later Bishop Waugh.

ENDNOTES

i   *Memoirs of a Senator from Pennsylvania* by Jonathan Roberts (1771–1854), The Pennsylvania Magazine of History and Biography, Vol. 62, No. 3 (July 1938), pp 361–409, Published by The Historical Society of Pennsylvania http://www.jstor.org/stable/20087129 Accessed 9/16/2012.

ii   *Doyle Family Papers 1793-1967. Section 3.* Mss1 D7784 a 8-15, Virginia Historical Society http://vhs4.vahistorical.org Accessed 9/26/2012.

iii *A Kind of Fate: Agricultural Change in Virginia, 1861-1920,* by G. Terry Sharrer, Purdue University Press, published in 2000.

iv http://en.wikipedia.org/wiki/Jacob_Hite Accessed 2/10/2014

v   Berkley County, Virginia, Will Book 1, available on Familysearch.com.

vi Per correspondent Nancy Bushby 31 Oct 2013, Land grant database has 1769 grant to Joseph Beeler of 751 acres on Opequon. Jacob may have purchased some of that land. Deed research would be required to verify the parcel.

vii *History of the First Baptist Church of Piscataway Stelton* by Oliver B. Leonard, Esq., Plainfield, NJ, 1889. A transcription of the Pioneer Biographie's section by K. Thorp on the Genealogy Trails Middlesex County website: http://genealogytrails.com/njer/middlesex/piscatawaypioneers.html accessed 2 20/2015.

viii   *History of Clay and Platte Counties, Missouri - Google eBook,* National Historical Company, 1885. Pages 1106 and 1107 contain a biography of their grandson John Talbot Martin.

ix   http://chapters.scarecrowpress.com/07/391/0739107208ch1.pdf *Religion in Colonial Virginia: A Brief Overview* Accessed 12/5/2012.

x   *Hite Family Homesteads: Neckar to Shenandoah* by Elizabeth Coles Umstattd, Hite Family Association p 84

xi   *The Descendants of the Rev. Nathaniel Manning, M.D. "Strictly a Family Affair"* by Louise Edrington Willis, June 1953, privately published but copies available from Alibris. This author has completely missed the fact that they had a second son, Nathaniel Manning, Jr.

xii   Mrs. Mattingly's Miracle by Nancy Lusignan Schultz, pp 186, 187quoted by permission from Ms. Schultz. This book cites *A History of the Valley of Virginia* by Samuel Kercheval, 1850, and History of Hardy County of the Borderland by Alvin Edward Moore, 1963 pp 66,67 as original references.

xiii   *The History of Hardy County, 1786–1986* by Richard K. McMaster, The Hardy County Public Library, 1986, page 86–88. See also *Early Fairfax Land Grants and Leases Along the South Branch of the* Potomac by Charles Morrison published in West Virginia History Vol. 37: 1–22 (Oct 1976). See http://www.wvgenweb.org/hardy/sbmanor.htm accessed 2/20/2015.

xiv   *The Hite Family and the Settlement of the West* by Richardson Hillier, Master's Thesis, University of Virginia, 1936, Chapter VI.

xv   *Journal of Isaac Hite, edited* by Virginius Hall, Bulletin of the Historical and Genealogical Society of Ohio, Cincinnati, Vol. 12 No. 4, pp 262–281, October 1954.

xvi   *The History of Hardy County, 1786–1986* by Richard K. McMaster, The Hardy County Public Library, 1986, page 86–88.

xvii   Berkeley County, West Virginia, Will Book I, accessed via familysearch, October 2013.

xviii   A History of Shenandoah County, Virginia as transmitted by Ellen Miller.

xix Jackson and Twohig's notes to the *Diaries of George Washington,* Vol. 4, p 51 (University Press of Virginia, 1978, available from Manuscript Division, Library of Congress through American Memory http://memory.loc.gov/ammem/gwhtml/gwhome.html accessed 2/9/2014.)

xx http://en.wikipedia.org/wiki/Jacob_Hite Accessed 2/10/2014.

xxi *Some Prominent Virginia Families.* Louise Pecquet du Bellet, Edward Jaquelin, Martha Cary Jaquelin. J. Bell & Co., Lynchburg, Virginia. 1901. p.350. Note, however, that they have his date of death wrong.

xxii *A Register of the General Assembly of Virginia 1776–1918,* by Earl G. Swem and John W. Williams, Richmond, 1918. https://archive.org/details/registerofgenera00virg Accessed 2/10/2014.

xxiii *The Wills of Berkeley County, Virginia,* Will Book 1. Available on familysearch.org

xxiv *Hite Family Homesteads: Neckar to Shenandoah,* by Elizabeth Madison Coles Umstattd, Hite Family Association Publishers; Revised edition (1997) Petition for Jacob's land in South Carolina resulted in land grants to the heirs; Mary received two 500 acre grants in 1784. Cited by Ellen Miller.

xxv Virginia Historical Society – *Isaac Hite Papers,* 1768–1798, of Mary's cousin Isaac Hite [1723–1795] of Frederick Co., VA. Includes accounts of Hite's activities as a merchant and iron manufacturer. Abraham Hite also owned an iron mine.

xxvi *Early Records, Hampshire County, Virginia* Clara McCormick Sage and Laura Sage Jones, Genealogical Publishing Company 1939, page 41. Plus research by Nancy Bushby.

xxvii Communication from Nancy Bushby.

xxviii Letter from Isaac Hite to Abraham Hite April 26, 1783 Special Collections Research Center, The Filson Historical Society Available on: http://memory.loc.gov/cgi-bin/query/r?ammem/fawbib:@field%28NUMBER+@band%28icufaw+cmf0003%29%29: Accessed 2/10/2014.

xxix *Washington and the West:* George Washington's diary of September, 1784; Archer B Hulburt, 1911.

xxx   Washington Papers - To George Washington from Abraham Hite, Jr., 29 January 1785. http://founders.archives. gov/documents/Washington/04-02-02-0216 Accessed 2/10/2014.

xxxi   Jackson and Twohig's notes to the *Diaries of George Washington,* Vol. 4, p 51, say they moved in 1788. (University Press of Virginia, 1978, available from Manuscript Division, Library of Congress through American Memory http://memory.loc. gov/ammem/gwhtml/gwhome.html accessed 2/9/2014.)

xxxii   An Inventory and Appraisement of the Estate of Thomas Hite brought to our view by Tavener Beale the 6th September 1779, Berkeley County, West Virginia, Will Book No. 1 pp 341–344.

xxxiii   Berkeley County, WV, Will Book No. 2, pp 57–66. Available in the Familysearch archive. Note that children were then called orphans when their father died even though the mother was still living.

xxxiv   *The Papers of James Madison Digital Edition,* J. C. A. Stagg, editor. Charlottesville: University of Virginia Press, Rotunda, 2010. http://rotunda.upress.virginia.edu/founders/JSMN-01-15-02-0158 [accessed 20 Oct 2013]

xxxv   *St. Louis Catholic Review* Volume II January, 1920, Number 1 Published by the Catholic Historical Society of Saint Louis 209 Walnut Street, St. Louis, Mo. Mary's first husband was named Edward Gerant, according to the 1804 court case.

xxxvi   Correspondence from Nancy Bushby.

xxxvii   Based on annotations to *The Journals and Letter of Francis Asbury* by Elmer T. Clark, J. Manning Potts, and Jacob S. Payton, Wesleyan Heritage Publications, 1998, plus a number of Internet sites such as http://www.owingsstone. com/getperson.php?personID=I13135&tree=owingsstone (accessed March 27, 2014).

xxxviii   *Journal of Rev. Francis Asbury, Bishop of the Methodist Episcopal Church,* Vol. 1 from August 7, 1771 to Dec. 31, 1786, published by Lane & Scott, New York, 1852, following page 461. As a matter of interest, Richard Williams was an ancestor of my correspondent, Nancy Bushby, and Asbury tells a fantastic story of his escape from Indians.

xxxix   In May 1785, Trinity Methodist church leaders arranged a personal interview with General George Washington at Mount Vernon for the Bishops Thomas Coke and Francis Asbury, who met at William Bushby's house in Alexandria before traveling on to meet with the General regarding the emancipation of slaves. Stukenbroeker, Fern C. 1974. *A Watermelon for God: a history of Trinity United Methodist Church, Alexandria, Virginia*, 1774-1974, p 22.

xl   A good example is Alexander White. In a 1793 letter to Madison, he admits to having being dubious but changing his mind later on.

xli   Madison originally wanted his bicameral legislatures both to be population based. He was forced to give more power to small states in composing the Senate and later decided this was for the best. *American Creation* by Joseph J. Ellis, Chapter Three, Vintage Books Random House, New York, 2007.

xlii   Reference (from Nancy Bushby) Fairfax County Deed Book R, pages 342–343 and Book S, pages 532–533.

xliii   All this is referred to in a letter from William Bushby to James Madison dated Sept., 24, 1805. http://memory.loc. gov/ammem/collections/madison_papers/mjmser1.html p994 accessed 2/6/2014.

xliv   *Shenandoah Valley Pioneers and their Descendants: A History of Frederick County Virginia* by Thomas Kemp Cartmell, 1909, The Eddy Press Corp., Winchester, VA.

xlv   *The James Madison Papers,* Library of Congress, American Memory.

xlvi   Found in *The James Madison Papers, Library of Congress, American Memory,* http://memory.loc.gov/ammem/ collections/madison_papers/ accessed in January 2014.

xlvii   Deed Book SC 3, p. 297 August 25, 1794, Frederick County, Winchester, VA.

xlviii   *Chronicles of the Scotch-Irish Settlement of Virginia*; Vol. 2, pp 140–149 "Defendants are, viz.: Edward Gerant and Mary, his wife; Theodrick Lee and _____, his children by his late wife Catherine, Sarah, wife of A. P. Buchanan. which said Mary, Catherine, and Sarah were daughters and heirs of John Hite, deceased, who was son and heir of Jacob Hite, deceased; and James Hite, Carver Willis and Frances, his wife, who are children and heirs of Thomas Hite, deceased, another devisee of Jacob; and William Boushby and Mary, his; wife, late Mary Manning, a devisee of Jacob."

xlix   Proceedings of the Commissioners, 10, 12 November 1796; Thomas Carbery to Commissioners, 1 March 1797, 6 May 1797, Letters Received; Commissioners to Carbery, 3 May 1797, Letters Sent, RDCC. Referred to in *At Peace with All Their Neighbors: Catholics and Catholicism in the National Capital, 1787–1860* The Estate of William W. Warner. (Kindle Location 4128). Kindle Edition.

l   Records of the Columbia Historical Society.

li   It took Mary's son-in-law, Jonathan Roberts, three days to make the trip in 1814 but that was in the middle of winter. The Pennsylvania Magazine of History and Biography, Vol. 62, No. 3 (Jul., 1938), pp.374–375.

lii   Source is Ellen Miller's family tree at Ancestry.com.

liii   Actual evidence is missing but three of their daughters married St. Mary's County Catholics living in Washington. Her biography indicates that Mary H. Manning, the eldest, attended a Catholic school, probably Visitation. The other girls probably did too. Census records indicate they were living away from home, perhaps at boarding school, after 1820. This Mary later married ex-Mayor Thomas Carbery.

liv   Source is Bronwen Souders' Essay on *Eudora*.

lv   Based on the fact that her son-in-law, a US Senator, never mentions these connections in his memoirs.

lvi   *Henry Clay and the War of 1812* by Quentin Scott King, McFarland, Feb 28, 2014 p 251.

lvii   *Memoirs of a Senator from Pennsylvania: Jonathan Roberts, 1771–1854, The Pennsylvania Magazine of History and Biography*, Vol. 62, No. 3 (Jul., 1938), pp.361–409 Published by: The Historical Society of Pennsylvania. (Other editions of the magazine carry other parts of his story.)

lviii   The letters of Edward Fitzgerald referred to here are to be found in the *Doyle Family Papers* 1793–1967 Section 3, Call No. D7784 a 8-15, at the Historical Society of Virginia.

lix   *A Story of Courage: Annals of the Georgetown Convent of the Visitation of the Blessed Virgin Mary* by George Parsons Lathrop and Rose Hawthorne Lathrop, Riverside Press, Cambridge, 1895.

lx   *Notes on Sister Mary Theonella Hite and Her Family* by Scannel O'Neill, St. Louis Catholic Review, Volume II, January,1920, Number 1, Published by the Catholic Historical Society of Saint Louis 209 Walnut Street, St. Louis, Mo.

lxi   *The Descendants of the Rev. Nathaniel Manning, M.D. "Strictly a Family Affair"* by Louise Edrington Willis, page 11.

lxii   *At Peace with All Their Neighbors: Catholics and Catholicism in the National Capital, 1787–1860* The Estate of William W. Warner. (Kindle Location 4128). Kindle Edition.

lxiii   *Mrs. Mattingly's Miracle: The Prince, the Widow, and the Cure That Shocked Washington City* by Nancy Lusignan Schultz, Yale University Press, 2011.

lxiv   *Historical and Biographical Record of Southern California* by James Miller Guinn, pp 235–237, Chapman Publishing Company, 1902.

lxv   *Mrs. Mattingly's Miracle page 187.*

lxvi   Communication from Nancy Bushby referring to "Petition 20482402. Records of the United States Circuit Court, Chancery Dockets and Rule Case Files, Record Group 21, Document #147, Box 22, Folder 20, Book 3. National Archives."

lxvii   *A Kind of Fate: Agricultural Change in Virginia, 1861–1920,* by G. Terry Sharrer, Purdue University Press, published in 2000.

lxviii   *Long Meadows* by Minnie Hite Moody, McMillan Company, 1941, pp 159,160. Others place the unmarked graves of Jost and his wife Anna Maria in the Old Opequan Cemetery (Presbyterian) in Kernstown or in the private family cemetery at Long Meadows. See http://www.findagrave.com/cgi-bin/ fg.cgi?page=gr&GRid=20847409 Accessed 2/10/2014. This latter reference gives the date of death as May 7, 1760, differing from most other authorities.

CPSIA information can be obtained
at www.ICGtesting.com
Printed in the USA
LVHW071336270120
644925LV00014B/459